FLORIDA SURVIVAL GARDENING

Other Books by David the Good

Compost Everything: The Good Guide to Extreme Composting

Grow or Die: The Good Guide to Survival Gardening

Push the Zone: The Good Guide to Growing Tropical Plants Beyond the Tropics

Free Food for Everyone: The Good Guide to Plant Propagation

Create Your Own Florida Food Forest

Totally Crazy Easy Florida Gardening

The Easy Way to Start a Home-Based Plant Nursery

The Survival Gardener's Guide to Growing Your Own Caffeine

The Survival Gardener's Guide to Growing Your Own Tobacco

Turned Earth: A Jack Broccoli Novel

FLORIDA SURVIVAL GARDENING

DAVID The GOOD

GOOD BOOKS

Florida Survival Gardening
David the Good

Cover: Matthew King

Good Books Publishing
goodbookspub.com

ISBN: 978-1-955289-05-4

Contents

DEDICATION

To all the Good Gardeners who support my work while sharing seeds, inspiration and friendship. Thank you—may we all get to meet one day.

INTRODUCTION

The Sunshine State is a great place to grow food during uncertain times. We have decent rainfall and an almost tropical climate which allows us to dip into the resources of both temperate and tropical climates, growing year-round if need be. You can literally grow thousands of pounds of food in the average Florida backyard, provided you are not afraid to work hard and tear up your pretty St. Augustine grass. Ignore the complaints about the sand, the heat and the bugs—once you know how to work around them, you will have marvelous success.

Back in 2015 I wrote *Totally Crazy Easy Florida Gardening: The Secret to Growing Piles of Food in the Sunshine State*. That book went on to become a regular best-seller in Amazon's "South Region Gardening" category, as well as making it far up the sales list into the heart of the main gardening category. The reason I wrote the book was to reveal what I'd discovered about Florida gardening success. The real key to "growing piles of food in the Sunshine State" is picking the crops that grow well in our unique climate, rather than fighting to grow things that we read about in gardening books from up north. One criticism I received was that some of the crops I mentioned were hard to find—and this is true, though over the past five years, many of the plants I recommend for Florida have become more widely available thanks to the great success many gardeners have had with them after reading my book.

For years I tested underutilized tropical crops such as chayote, chaya, maize, jicama, yard-long beans, true yams, longevity spinach, *Abelmoschus manihot*, and others, planting them alongside my regular staples like sweet potatoes, black-eyed peas, collards, and cabbages then seeing how well they grew in Florida. My thought was, "Hey, if they grow in countries with high humidity, lots of heat, and lots of insects, maybe they'll thrive here!" And many of them did. Based on that success, I created a list of "Totally Crazy Easy" crops for Florida, then wrote a book on my methods and recommendations. Since then, many people have sent me their thanks for writing a book that finally made Florida gardening accessible to beginners and not only doable, but easy!

Totally Crazy Easy Florida Gardening was not primarily focused on food security, however. In it I recommend you try various methods and test as you go along, learning and growing with your garden. Later, in 2016, I wrote *Grow or Die: The Good Guide to Survival Gardening*, which compiled a lot of information I had gathered on survival gardening and meshed it with my own experience feeding my family. It has also gone on to be a best-seller. As I write this new book, it has moved back up into the top 1000 books sold on Amazon. *Grow or Die*'s main focus was broader than Florida, however, and it was purposefully designed to cover a range of climates. It covers a range of methods depending on location and what the gardener prefers to do, from deep-mulching to raised beds.

The focus of this book is just on survival gardening in Florida. Consider it a crash-course in feeding your family in the Sunshine State. I will share exactly what I would do to feed my family as best as possible from a small Florida backyard. My recommendations are based on experience with pests and heat and sand and a wide variety of tropical staple crops. My hope for you is that you will lose your fear and take charge of the land you have, harnessing it to grow you enough to keep you fed for a long time, no matter what happens in the world. We'll handle this together.

Chapter 1

GETTING STARTED WITH SIMPLE GARDEN BEDS

Throw out what you "know" about vegetable gardening. It's no longer the time for cutesy hobby gardens and there's no need to hit the hardware store for lumber before you plant a bed of salad greens.

Raised beds with wooden boundaries are not the best way to garden in Florida sand. Northern gardeners are always recommending them, but they are unnecessary and not practical for most survival gardening applications in Florida. Raised beds heat the soil up faster and drain faster, requiring more watering. Sure, there are fancy ways to fight this, like putting rotten wood in the bottom when you make your bed, or adding lots of compost, or drip irrigation—and of course, they look pretty, but we're survival gardening here, not trying to win a *Better Homes & Gardens* competition. All you really need to do is to dig up a portion of your yard and make lightly mounded beds with paths in between.

Don't worry. Your dirt beds are going to look great when they're covered with plants. They're also going to be a lot easier to weed than raised beds, as you can move your hoe through the paths and beds without weeds and grass getting jammed up against the wood sides of the beds.

Here's how to start a brand-new garden the cheap and easy way.

Pick Your Space

Pick a space that gets at least 4 hours of sun per day. Florida gardens get more sun than they need—it's HOT here! Morning sun is better than afternoon sun, if your yard allows it. A garden that gets full sun until noon will be fine if oak shadows cover it for the afternoon. Full sun is fine, though. It's just harder to keep some things growing into summer.

Do not pick a swampy spot or an area that floods, as it will drown plant roots. You can grow other edible things in wet areas, such as tannia, bananas, dasheen, and water spinach, but most vegetables will not be happy. If a wet area is all you have, make higher mounds with small "canals" in between to drain away excess water so you can grow regular garden vegetables.

To get started on a garden, remove all the vegetation you can from your intended plot. String-trim or mow the area down to bare ground. If you own a tiller or can borrow or rent one, just till up the entire space. If you do not have a tiller and/or prefer to work with hand tools, you can use a broadfork or a spading fork to loosen all the area, including paths, then pull the weed roots up in handfuls. Throw them some place to dry out in the sun so they can be later fed into the compost pile without re-rooting.

Now mark off the first bed using stakes and twine. Though it's not truly necessary and the plants won't know if you make an uneven bed, there is a certain satisfaction that comes from good straight lines and rows of beds lined up like soldiers. My beds are mostly 4' wide and as long as I like. Usually, I don't make them much longer than 25' or so without ending them in a path that lets me get to the next set of beds without stepping in a bed. In between your 4' wide beds, mark out 2' wide paths. Rebar makes great stakes for running string, though sticks or pieces of wood work fine too. If you are planning to dig more than one bed, mark off all the space for the beds and paths.

This part is fun, as it allows you to really see your garden layout before it's finished. If you'd rather not bother with stakes and string, that's fine too. Just do your best to create 4' wide beds and leave 2' wide paths in between them.

When you fork up your beds, they'll be nice and loose and a little taller than the surrounding ground, unless you have very loose sugar sand. I used to think it didn't matter much if I dug up the sand, but I found through experimentation that even sand can get compacted and airless and will grow better plants with some loosening, especially if you throw down some compost before loosening, which allows it to fall down into the cracks as you dig and fork. If you don't have a fork or a tiller, just turn the ground over with a shovel. One with a small, light head is easier to manage than a big, heavy square shovel. Take small bites and try to get out the remaining weeds, roots and rocks as you go.

To mark out paths and to facilitate drainage in heavy rains, rake some of the loose soil out of the paths and onto the beds, making low mounds. And once your beds are nice and loose, don't step on them!

The reason for 2' pathways in between beds is so you can easily pick and harvest and push a wheelbarrow through your gardens. If you are really short on space, however, you can go down to 16" between beds, though any smaller than that and it gets uncomfortably crowded, especially if children, spouses, or pets are following on your heels.

As you are building your beds, it makes sense to add in compost if you have it. You do not need a ton—just a quarter inch to a half-inch or so on top of each bed, raked or dug in. If you do not have compost, you may find some in the woods under leaf litter. And start a pile today! Other good amendments include wood ashes, cottonseed meal, greensand, coffee grounds, chicken or rabbit manure, kelp meal, crushed eggshells, alfalfa pellets or meal, or even some chicken feed or dog food. Just dig some of what you have into each bed as you go. Don't add too much chicken manure or dog food, though, as both of those are high in nitrogen. And if you have lots of pest critters in your area, skip the dog food. It really is a great fertilizer, but it will sometimes attract unwanted visitors. If you have nothing to feed your new beds, don't worry. I have some innovative feeding solutions that will help you keep crops happy—we'll cover those in an upcoming chapter where we'll cover all the amendments you'll ever need.

Digging in amendments when you make your beds will put some nutrition in the root zone of your plants that they can find as they grow.

Unfortunately, I can no longer recommend cow, horse, or other ruminant manures as most of them are contaminated with long-term herbicides (look up "Aminopyralid") used to control weeds—they'll often kill your garden before it even gets a good start. Multiple Florida gardeners have told me they lost entire years because of spreading around manure or rotten hay.

As I wrote in *Compost Everything: The Good Guide to Extreme Composting*:

[D]on't import manure for your garden if:

1. *The source farm isn't organic*

2. *The animals are eating imported feed/hay or living in imported bedding straw*

3. *The animals are treated with chemical de-wormers/antibiotics/etc.*

4. *A bagged manure/compost contains "biosolids"*

As you'll quickly see from that list it's basically impossible to meet those criteria. Yet if you don't, you're running the risk of poisoning your ground. It's just not safe to add manure anymore unless you know it's safe.... Don't bring manure, compost, straw, or grass clippings onto your property. Trust no one except people that don't feed their animals any purchased hay and who you are sure do not spray their fields with anything. This is the only way to be completely sure your garden won't get whacked. Look, I'm not hyper cautious, but this is deadly stuff, and it sticks around in the ground. It's been years since I got hit and many of my perennials never recovered. The supply chains are really long. It's really hard to find out where hay and straw originally came from. Chances are, a lot of it is being sprayed.

Aminopyralids don't hurt grasses, so they're often used on wheat, corn, grains, and pastures. In the name of convenience and saving time, they're poisoning the supply chain for organic farmers. Once you know about the existence of these long-term pesticides and the range of their use, you'll look sideways at a lot of amendments that used to be perfect for your garden. The game has changed. Don't get nailed.

I wish I could say to go ahead and get that trailer of rotten horse manure and spread it, but chances are now quite high that you'll wreck your gardens. It's happened again and again to many of my readers and viewers. Manure is no longer worth the risk of Aminopyralid contamination. If you've ever grown a garden and had your plants start growing in weird twisting shapes, then dying over a few weeks or months without producing, that's likely what happened to you. One friend spread rotten hay over her food forest as mulch and it wrecked a lot of her plants. Another person told me they grew great melons for years with tilled-in horse manure, then suddenly had a year where they spread manure and everything died. There you go—it's out there, and it's not safe. It's also getting into the bagged manure market, as well as the compost you can purchase, and even into garden soil mixes. The great irony is that your garden is *safer* when you use 10-10-10 or MiracleGro than if you use one of the best traditional garden amendments! What a topsy-turvy world.

Enough about contaminated manure. Back to beds.

4' wide beds work well for most crops. For cassava and true yams, however, I make low mounds 2' wide with 1–2' paths in between. For pumpkins, just dig up a big area and plant on hills with about 8' between hills in all directions. For sweet potatoes, you can loosen the ground and plant slips 16" or so apart in rows 3' apart.

Now that you have your garden beds dug, it's time to start planting.

Seeds and Transplants

Direct-seeding in the garden is my preferred way to grow. It makes for stronger seedlings that are adapted to the garden environment. Transplants are usually grown under ideal conditions, with a little shade and in perfect soil with plenty of water. When placed into the garden, they are shocked by the harsher conditions and can sometimes take longer to produce than plants that were started directly from seed in place.

South Florida is a better place for direct-seeding, as you aren't as tied to the calendar since there are very few frosts to worry about. In North Florida, you have to work around frost dates—and then it gets hot, hot, hot a little while later, causing many of your cool-season plants to give up. Starting peppers, moringa, tobacco, amaranth, sunflowers, and Everglades tomatoes early makes sense. It may also make sense to grow cabbages, brassicas and lettuces in trays a bit early. Start cool-season vegetables in trays in December and January for February plantings. Start warm-season vegetables that cannot withstand frost in January and February for a head start. It's important to start warm-season vegetable transplants in a warm location. If the soil is cold—even if not freezing—warm season vegetable seeds just sit and won't germinate until the soil warms up. Sometimes they just rot and never come up at all. Moringa seeds, for instance, don't like to germinate unless the soil is good and warm. When I ran my plant nursery, I used heat mats to give seeds the warm soil they needed to grow. If you have a small greenhouse, so much the better—but that's quite a bit more complicated and expensive.

Many garden plants do not like transplanting, such as corn, beans, carrots, melons, pumpkins, beets, turnips, and radishes. Better to direct-sow. Large-seeded plants often do better direct-seeded as they are less likely to get buried too deeply or destroyed in the soil by various critters. Tomatoes, peppers, lettuce, and brassicas don't mind transplanting all that much. Plastic transplant trays are cheap. You don't need ones with plastic tops, you don't need peat pots or anything fancy. Just a multi-celled tray. Even less fancy, you can just make a box out of scrap lumber with slats or a piece of ply on the bottom with holes drilled through it for drainage. Pressure-treated 1x4's make for a good flat, as do pallet boards, though they don't last as long. I wouldn't make wooden flats bigger than 16" x 16" as they get heavy. I hired my twelve-year-old to make ten planting flats for me and they've gotten plenty of use this year.

Planting flats should be filled with good potting soil that doesn't have any added fertilizer. If you cannot get potting soil, you can make your own by crumbling up rotten wood and mixing it with sand and finished compost. You're more likely to get some damping off issues with homemade potting soil, however. (Damping-off is where seedling stems spontaneously rot from an infection.)

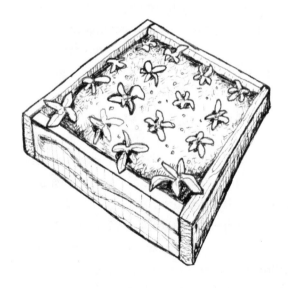

A simple homemade wooden flat for transplants.

If you have new seed from a reputable company, plant one seed per cell in a multi-cell tray, or plant one seed every inch in your wooden planting flat. If your seed is older or cheap, plant 2–4 seeds in the same space. Keep the trays watered well so they don't dry out, but do not keep them soaked as that can make seeds and seedlings rot. Most seedlings are ready for transplanting when they're a couple inches tall and have their true leaves. I let moringa grow to six inches or more before transplanting.

If you set aside a small nursery area—under the dappled light of a thin tree or on a patio is good—you can start transplants and seeds and do grafting and other experiments and always have plants ready to go into the garden. Currently I am growing a wide range of things for my vegetable gardens and my food forests. Right now my nursery area is growing pots and flats of pomegranates, cocoplums, tiger amaranth, large red cherry tomatoes, tabasco peppers, chocolate pudding fruit, pink bananas, limeberries, black Surinam cherries, Barbados cherries, zinnias, marigolds, cauliflower, red Russian kale, tobacco, ice cream beans, coffee, and who knows what else. When you start your own plants, you always have something to put into gaps as they arise—and to give away or trade with other gardeners. It is a lot of fun to keep a little nursery area going and it's well worth the small amount of time it takes to set one up.

We could talk about exciting exotic plants all day, but we need to get back to the serious business of survival gardening. Now that have our beds dug and have covered transplants and seeds, let's learn how to grow the serious survival staples that make sense in Florida.

Chapter 2

STAPLE SURVIVAL CROPS FOR FLORIDA

If this were a normal gardening book, we'd talk about lettuces and beefsteak tomatoes, asparagus, and summer squash. But it isn't. This is a survival gardening book and the "main" crops most of us plant when we have a hobby garden are not the main crops we would grow for survival. You will get awfully hungry trying to subsist on cucumbers and jalapeños. I still plant a few because they are wonderful and help provide some variety to our meals, but the first order of business is to plant calorie-dense crops.

It is important to grow your calories first, then your nutrition crops. You want a full stomach! Starchy crops like potatoes, bananas, sweet potatoes, cassava, true yams (*Dioscorea spp.*), beans, maize/grain corn, Seminole pumpkins and calabaza squash, sunflowers, and turnips are your high-calorie allies. After those, plant high-nutrition plants like moringa, longevity spinach, kale, chaya, collards, etc. Most of your leafy greens will only grow well in spring and fall, and the same goes for some of your calorie crops. In the heat of summer, you are mostly limited to planting chaya, yard-long green beans, black-eyed peas, okra, and sweet potatoes. Some of the crops I mentioned may not be familiar to you, such as chaya and true yams, but there are gardeners who can share propagative material with you in the state, and you can find true yams at Publix sold as "name" yams, pronounced "nah-may".

In this chapter, I will take you through some sure-fire calorie crops first and share growing details, then in the next chapter we'll go through the nutrition crops, followed by a look at a few additional plants that are worth growing if you still have space.

Bananas/Plantains

Bananas and plantains are easy to grow in South Florida, moderately easy to grow in central Florida, and slower and harder to grow in North Florida due to freezing temperatures in winter. In the tropics, you can basically live on bananas and plantains. Ripe, they are sweet and delicious. Bananas are good off the stalk and ripe plantains are good fried, baked or roasted in a fire. If you pick bananas or plantains green, they can be peeled and boiled, added to stews, boiled and mashed into a porridge with sugar and spices, or sliced and fried in oil. It's like the best of a root crop and the best of a fruit crop.

Some banana trees mature quite rapidly and produce fruit within a year of planting if well-fed and watered. Others take a bit longer. The key to bananas is regular feeding and watering. They love to sit next to seeping water. I had excellent luck running my sink drain into a stand of bananas.

This banana pup is growing vigorously from the remnants of a large bullhead.

As denizens of the rainy tropics, bananas thrive on more water than Florida gets from the sky. It's estimated that they like around 100 inches of water per year, which is roughly twice the rainfall Florida gets. If they are not watered, they grow slowly and may spend years without fruiting. This is what happened with the unirrigated bananas in my North Florida yard and in my parents' South Florida food forest. Their thirstiness makes sense when you cut down a banana stalk. It's like a huge column of water held together with tough fibers. Bananas really like to drink.

To start bananas, it is necessary to take donor plant material from an existing stand of trees. Get a sharp shovel or your trusty machete and dig out a "pup" tree from alongside the main clump, making sure you get the bulb at the bottom. Shoot for a pup that is roughly 4' tall. Smaller pups take longer to grow and produce. If you chop off the stem and don't get the roots, it will die. Alternatively, you can chop down a larger non-fruiting stalk to a foot or so from the ground and dig out the stump, separating it from the main clump of banana trees, then plant that. Big trunk sections with a large piece of root mass are called "bull heads" and will make a few small trees that shoot up quickly and often grow faster than transplanted pups.

When you plant bananas, give them a space in full sun if possible, though they can still fruit in half sun. In North Florida, plant them along the south side of buildings or close to warm walls and water tanks so they have an easier time on freezing nights. Dig a nice hole and throw in a handful or two of wood ashes if you have them, then plant banana pups at about the same depth they were before. Some people plant a couple of bananas next to each other in each station to help create a sheltered microclimate. Plant larger banana and plantain varieties at about 8–10' apart. Dwarf types, like the diminutive Dwarf Cavendish, can be planted at about 5–6' apart. Mulch around the newly planted trees and don't let the weeds crowd them or vines cover them. Feed with lots of nitrogen. Peeing at the base of the trees a few times a week is a Florida Gardening Best Practice™. They also like plenty of compost, some chicken manure, or high-nitrogen fertilizers. A generous sprinkling of wood ashes now and again helps provide potassium, which as we all know is one of the nutrients provided by what may be "the world's most perfect fruit", as the old ad put it. Alternatively, you can feed them with a high-potassium commercial fertilizer. Fertilizer is marked with three numbers representing Nitrogen, Phosphorus and Potassium (NPK). If the third number (K) is high, that is what bananas like.

Bananas are not a quick crop like beans or cabbage. They will take some time to get established and start producing, often a couple of years. Once they start to make a clump and spread, the fruit will start coming with regularity and you'll get plenty of calories for only a little work. They also like some shelter from wind. Bananas in full sun and wind in the middle of a field alone will suffer greatly. It's better for them to have eastern exposure rather then western if they aren't in an all-day sun location. They also love humidity, which is why it's good to plant bananas near each other to hold in some moisture and shade the ground.

The largest stalk in a clump will go into bloom when it's ready. A large, heart-shaped inflorescence emerges from the crown of the stalk and starts moving downward, unfurling and making bananas as it goes. The bananas are the female blooms. After the tree finishes making those, the inflorescence keeps moving down, making male blooms. These attract insects and hummingbirds but will not make bananas. When the bananas on the stalk grow nice and fat and start to turn a light dull green color, you can cut them down. Or you can wait until the first few bananas turn yellow and cut the stalk down.

Once cut, the bananas will ripen rapidly—sometimes faster than you can eat them. If need be, freeze extras to store for the future. Or cook some of the green bananas as if they were potatoes and eat the ripe ones out of hand. Plantains usually need cooking to be palatable, even when ripe and yellow. I like them when they start getting black spots and are soft when squeezed. You'll get a feel for it over time. My brother-in-law Tyler is half Puerto-Rican and he fries them before they turn sweet, cutting them into rounds and smashing them flat with a spatula in oil, getting them nice and crispy and then salting them. They are delicious that way.

Once a banana "tree" has produced a stalk of bananas, it's done. Cut it down to the ground and chop it up to use as mulch or compost. Once it's out of the way, other stalks in the clump will fruit and new pups will replace it. Over time, one banana tree will grow into a clump of bananas and eventually into a big stand of bananas. They will not be as productive this way, however. It's better to cut down the big stalks after they fruit and remove all but 1–2 of the other stalks around it to encourage the plant to make more fruit rather than more stalks. You can always chop out a few pups to plant elsewhere or give away if you feel bad about paring down the clump.

Bananas love organic matter and rich soil. Florida often lacks both, so be sure to keep your bananas happy by mulching them and throwing in whatever humus-building material you have. Old coffee grounds, grass clippings, kitchen scraps—just throw them in and around the clumps to rot down. When you're chopping down weeds or stripping vines off the fence, just feed them to the banana monster.

Another method for growing bananas is to create a "banana circle", as I wrote about in *Compost Everything*:

Permaculture enthusiasts in tropical to subtropical climates love making a specialized type of garden/compost pile called a 'banana circle'. The basic concept is simple: bananas crave water and are voracious feeders that love lots of organic matter. In order to hold on to water and nutrition, make a roughly yard-deep circular indentation in the ground. Angle it to trap runoff, leaving one end open to the flow of water across your property, or run a drainpipe off your roof, set up an outdoor shower or urinal, or do what I did: run the water from the kitchen sink out of the house. Around the edges of that pit, mound up the dirt taken from the center. You will be planting your bananas in the edge mound along with other plants that will benefit from the soon-to-be moist conditions and high fertility of the circle.

Where does the fertility come from? That's the fun part! In the middle of your newly dug circle, start dumping a lot of organic matter. Chunks of log, straw, manure, kitchen scraps, chopped weeds, Spanish moss, fish guts, coffee grounds, sugarcane waste, feathers, newspapers, and whatever else you can find. Make a nice big mound; it will rot down quickly. After you've done that, mulch well over the bare soil, and start planting on the berm around the pile in the center. Bananas are the keystone of this design, so plant them first, and then start adding plants in between. Toward the center, where the soil will be more damp, add moisture-loving plants such as cannas, malanga, or taro. At the top of the berm, consider planting lemongrass, comfrey, sage, yacon, and other species that don't mind it drier. On the outside of the berm, try planting cassava, chaya, squash, and other edibles. A ground cover of sweet potatoes is often recommended, as that adds one more layer of edibility to the design, and the rapidly growing vines keep weeds under control. As you plant, make sure to leave a gap in the edge of the circle so you can continue to throw organic matter on the compost heap in the center. This system will digest a remarkable amount of organic matter while paying you back in food.

Which reminds me, I need to build another one of those where my washing machine drains. They sure grow some impressive bananas.

When temperatures drop in the fall and winter, bananas quit growing. They love days in the 80s and wet weather, but cold and dry weather makes them slow down or stop altogether. Frosts will kill the fruit and foliage and will sometimes kill the trunks right to the ground. However, this isn't always the case. North Florida gardeners often remove all the brown leaves or chop the trunks off after a freeze, making the plants regrow from lower down. I do not recommend this! If it's winter and you get a freeze that toasts your banana trees, just leave them alone. I don't care how ugly they look—leave them alone until spring. The dead leaves will help keep the remaining trunks warm in case of a further freeze. In spring once the danger of frost has passed, you can go ahead and take off the dead leaves, but don't attack the trunks right away. Wait and see what happens. Often, a new leaf will emerge from the top and the tree will keep on growing. If you chop it all down to make it look nice, you won't get fruit as quickly. If the trunks get rotten and start to collapse, go ahead. Otherwise, wait and see. An exception is if a stalk was already blooming when Jack Frost arrived. If the bloom and/or young bananas are toasted, cut the whole stalk down—it's done. You'll have to wait for the next "tree" to produce.

Beans

Beans are a good survival staple if you grow them to the dry stage. Dry beans are not super productive for the space they take up, though they are worth growing for their protein content and how they improve the soil for subsequent crops. I grew multiple varieties of beans in North Florida over the years and had problems with getting dry beans. Green beans? No problem! But not dry beans. This is due to Florida's weather and how beans grow. Beans are a warm season crop that cannot take frost, so they are commonly planted in Central/North Florida in March/April and will make beans in June/July, leading to dry beans in the middle of the summer rainy season. This means that as the plants are starting to dry, the monsoons come and soak the pods repeatedly leading to moldy and sometimes sprouting "dry" beans. In South Florida you'll probably have better luck letting them dry down outdoors as you can plant beans in the fall and winter and harvest them during the dry weeks of winter. I did have luck in North Florida growing black-eyed peas and mung beans to the dry stage. They seem to resist the rain better than the other varieties I tried, like the classic "Jacob's Cattle" soup bean. That said, I have since done an experiment with picking an entire bean plant when the pods are filled out and getting rubbery, then taking it inside and hanging up the entire plant by the roots to dry. This gives me decent dry beans, though younger green pods on uprooted plants will not amount to anything.

Runner beans simply refused to make me more than a few pods so I gave up on them. Limas also failed regularly on me. So, though I am listing beans here as a caloric staple, not all beans are created equal and not all will make good dry beans for you. In the green stage, however, most beans are a reliable and easy-to-grow vegetable.

Beans come in a wide range of varieties and types, ranging from annuals to perennials, bush to pole, soup beans, green beans, long beans, and more. Bush types support themselves on short vines and bear quicker than pole types, but they are less productive (some estimates say pole beans produce twice as much as bush types) and a little touchier, though they're still one of the easiest vegetables to grow. If you can manage to get dry beans, they are quite valuable as a staple due to their high starch and protein content. Green beans, unfortunately, are quite low in calories, so they don't make the "calorie crop" cut.

Beans are a warm season crop and should go in the garden after all danger of frost, but not once things have gotten super hot (with the exception of yard-long beans and black-eyed peas, which will grow no matter what the heat is outside). To grow bush varieties, plant in rows 16" apart with your beans about 6" apart in the rows. That gives you three rows in one of your 4' wide beds. Beans can take crowding a lot better than some other crops. Mung and some black-eyed peas are bush types, as are most black beans. "Contender" beans are a good green bean as well as a decent soup bean. It's become a favorite on our homestead, with better flavor than Tendergreen and Kentucky Wonder. There are many beans which are supposed to have excellent flavor when dry, though I usually do not have enough space to plant a lot of dry beans and my North Florida garden was not kind to the more exotic varieties I tried.

We are currently growing a few rows of black beans right now which we will grow until the beans have filled out and the pods are leathery, then pull the entire plants up and hang them indoors to dry and mature.

Beans need little or no fertilization unless the soil is really dead. They benefit from moderately fertile soil and regular water. The beans I planted by my grey water drain make a lot more pods than the ones out in the field that only get watered once or twice a week.

Pole beans need support to grow, as they'll vine to a height of 10' or so if you let them. Without support, they scramble on the ground and produce poorly. My favorite method for trellising is to cut pieces of 5/8" rebar to 8' in length, then hammer them 2' deep into the ground, placing them up to 16' or so apart. I then tie a piece of paracord or other rope from the top of one to the top of the other, getting it tight, but not so tight it pulls them down. I tie another piece of paracord at about 1' over the ground from one piece of rebar to the other. Then I tied strings from the top piece of paracord to the bottom at regular intervals and plant beans beneath them. Alternatively, cattle panels make very good bean trellises. Or you can make bean teepees with three long sticks tied at the top. Plant 3 or 4 beans at the base of each pole and let the beans climb to the middle. In a pinch, you can just ram individual sticks into the ground for each bean. Or let them grow on your chainlink fence, so long as the neighbor is okay with that.

Green beans are a very nice addition to your daily meals and are quite good when raw from the garden, dipped in homemade dressing, or eaten right off the bush. To grow bush varieties, plant in rows 16" apart with your beans about 6" apart in the rows. Beans can take crowding a lot better than some other crops. The first variety of bean I ever grew was Burpee's "Golden Wax" bean, which has bright yellow pods. It's not a particularly tasty variety, but I still grow it for nostalgia's sake.

As for pole types, Kentucky Wonder beans are easy to grow and produce well, though the best green bean I have grown in Florida is the "yard-long bean", also known as the "snake bean". They are a very productive and heat tolerant bean when picked green, though the dry beans are thin and not good for much other than planting. The hyacinth bean (also known as the lablab bean) can be cooked green as a shell bean, but I have only grown them once. Another round is coming up in my gardens right now. The yields are high, but the beans must be boiled when green as they are toxic raw. When fully ripe—that is, hard and dry—Green Deane recommends soaking them overnight, then boiling them, throwing out the water, then boiling them again to remove toxic glucosides. I have not tried this, but it is a staple crop in Asia, so I will try them that way this year. We shelled green beans from the pods when they filled out, boiled them for a long time, and ate them with no ill effects. However, the foliage on the vines is scratchy and may sting you if your skin is sensitive. That said, the foliage is also edible when boiled, and the root can be dug, boiled, and eaten as a starch. Lablab beans are very vigorous and easy to grow with high yields and lots of beautiful purple flowers. Give them a good trellis, as they are monster vines. If you cannot find seeds for sale in packets, try looking in the dry bean section of an Indian or Asian market and planting what you find. Often, dry beans will germinate from the store. That is how I am growing mung, black beans, and limas (trying again—I love limas!) right now.

As a final word on beans: in a survival situation, dry beans are the best for protein and calories, though North Florida gardeners will not have the easiest time of it. At least you'll get green beans.

Canna Lilies

Canna lilies are not something I have grown as a crop, per se, but they do have a very good starchy root. I planted clumps of them all over my North Florida food forest and they're a good source of hidden calories most thieves would never recognize as edible. Dig a clump and cook the roots in stews. There are a lot of strings in them you'll have to pull out after chewing, but hey—if you're hungry, it's good to know you can eat your landscaping. Some varieties are deliberately grown for their roots, but we ate the regular large-flowered orange ones now and again and they were good to eat. Cannas are a very low-maintenance flower that you can tuck in anywhere and eat them if you have to. The blooms are also edible and taste quite nice. Do not mix cannas up with calla lilies! The latter are poisonous.

Cannas like half-shade and decent soil and water. If it freezes they'll die back and reemerge in spring when temperatures warm back up. You can propagate non-seeded varieties by dividing the clumps. Seeded types have very hard round seeds that Green Deane compares to buckshot. I got very rapid and high germination rates by nicking them with nail clippers and soaking them overnight, then planting them in a flat of moist potting soil.

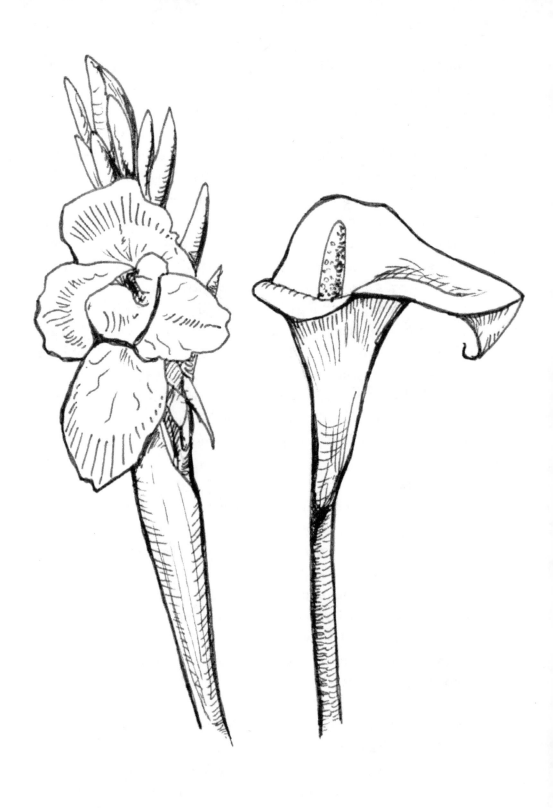

Left: the edible canna lily. Right: the poisonous calla lily.

Cassava

Cassava is a serious staple crop. It is low maintenance and more filling than anything else in this entire book. It's got about twice the amount of calories as regular white potatoes and also has nutrition-rich leaves which are edible after boiling for 20 minutes.

Cassava is a true tropical crop and is not happy in cold weather. I grew it in North Florida, but it would freeze to the ground in winter and took eighteen months to make decent-sized roots. When I grew it in warmer Frostproof, it produced roots within a year and grew through the winter without issue. When you read about cassava, you'll read that it contains cyanide and that there are both "sweet" and "bitter" varieties, the latter being very high in cyanide and only edible with extensive processing. That's not the type you want to grow. Stick to the "sweet" types, which is probably all you'll find in Florida anyhow, as the "bitter" types are usually used for commercial starch production rather than home gardening.

Spanish-speakers know cassava as "yuca". Caribbean islanders know it as cassava or manioc. Jamaicans, Puerto Ricans, various islanders, Indians, and Central Americans often have cassava to share or know where you can get planting material. Grower Jim in Orlando usually has it as well, as do permaculture gardeners and other eccentrics around the state. I got my first cassava cuttings from an older missionary who got his from Indian friends, then I grew the plants for years and shared it with many friends.

Do not confuse "yuca" with "yucca", despite what the spell-check on your stupid phone tells you. "Yucca" is an unrelated species and not even close to cassava, despite the similar name.

To grow cassava, plant 10–16" mature pieces of cassava stem in mounded banks of loose soil, 3–4' apart. Bury them about half-way into the ground so the top of the stem is sticking out, then water them in. If you have drier conditions, the stem cuttings may be buried diagonally or even on their sides a couple inches beneath the ground. They sprout slower that way but grow well.

If they are happy and warm, you will have roots in a year. I know people say "six months", but unless you find a fast-producing variety, you have to be a wizard to pull that off in most of Florida due to the cool season and lack of rain in spring and fall.

Propagative material isn't all that easy to find, even for the long season types. After a year, do some archaeology around the roots, digging carefully, to find the roots. They grow in spokes out from the central stem. If you have good-sized roots (2" diameter or so, or larger), chop the bush down and carefully pull them up from the sand. Be careful not to damage the roots as you dig around the plant. They are easy to chop through with a shovel. Once you have your roots, it is easy to make a slit in the sides about a quarter-inch deep and peel off the other bark layer, then cut the roots open and remove the woody threads in the very middle of each. Once dug, cassava roots only keep for a few days before starting to darken and spoil inside, so dig them when you need them or leave them in the ground. You can sneak a root or two from the sides of a growing plant if you do not want to dig the whole thing, but generally I just dig a plant all at once, peel the roots, plant the canes I cut down, then give the clean roots to my wife so she can cut them up and remove the woody centers and cook them.

Boil cassava in an open pot until it is soft, then it is safe to eat. Do not eat the raw roots, as they contain some cyanide precursors that are removed by boiling. The leaves can also be boiled for twenty minutes and eaten. Younger leaves are more tender, but all of them are a bit papery, though high in protein and nutrients. Recently we put some through the blender then cooked them into a soup. It was edible.

A good-sized cassava patch is excellent food security, especially if you are regularly replanting. The plants suffer from few issues in Florida and can be planted whenever you like as it is a non-seasonal crop. It grows much faster in warm weather and when the rain is falling, but it will tolerate cool days

Vertical, diagonal and horizontal cassava planting methods.

and dry weather. In winter, it makes sense to plant canes on their sides a couple inches deep to protect them from frost. I've found that it will spring up just fine when the soil warms, even if planted months earlier. In colder areas of the state, above-ground growth will freeze down but comes back in spring. This is a top survival crop if you can get planting material. Once you have some plants, you can always make more.

Roots from the store are unlikely to grow—stem cuttings are the best. If you can feed your cassava with a balanced fertilizer or compost it will do better than if it is just left to its own devices. It also seems to appreciate being mulched.

If you live in North Florida and want planting material for spring, cut canes down before the first frost. Then dig a pit and put some straw or leaves in it and carefully fill it up with longer pieces of cane, then cover with more leaves and straw and a layer of dirt or a tarp. You can dig them up in spring to plant out after all danger of frost. They'll keep beneath the ground just fine and may even start rooting and sprouting for you.

Corn/Maize

Sweet corn is not a good survival crop, but maize or "grain corn" varieties are. They produce calories fast and are one of the few grains that makes sense to grow on a small scale. Timing is important with corn as it does not thrive in the full heat and bugs of Florida summers, with the possible exception of coastal areas and the Southern portions of the state that do not get as brutal as the middle of the state during July and August. Plant in February/March in the Central to Northern part of the state and try growing it through the fall, winter and spring in the Southern part of the state. Some varieties are more suited to Florida than others. Dent corn types can take the Southern heat. One of my favorites is Hickory King for its excellent flavor when made into grits, but there are many others that will thrive. Corn can be planted in rows 24" apart with plants 6" apart in the rows, but if you have low rainfall or do not want to irrigate, plant them at roughly 36" apart with the seeds 1' or so apart inside the rows. Do not plant single rows of corn as corn is wind pollinated and needs multiple individuals around each plant to set full ears. Without good pollination, you'll get a lot of half-filled ears and skips inside the ears, or almost no corn at all. Another method is to make stations 4' apart in all directions, then plant 4 kernels of corn in each one. Dig a little hole and throw in some chicken manure or turf fertilizer or compost or fish guts or whatever in the bottom, then cover and plant over that. Plant seeds 1–2" deep and keep them watered well until they germinate. The closeness of the plants to each other helps ensure pollination and fruit set. If you plant on stations, you can run pumpkins or sweet potatoes or plant other vegetables in between the corn clumps. As corn grows, it is hungry for nitrogen. Feed it with urine diluted about 6 parts water to one part urine, or sprinkle a little high-nitrogen fertilizer around the plants when they are about 6" tall. Do not give them too much chemical fertilizer all at once as they will burn. Corn also likes a good dose of Dave's Fetid Swamp Water (recipe in an upcoming chapter) every week or two as it grows.

When the ears fill out nicely, you can pick them for roasted or boiled corn, which is like corn on the cob but not as sweet. When the husks brown, and the kernels get hard, take them inside and peel back the husks to let the kernels dry completely. Now you can use them for grinding or parching. Store them someplace dry and safe from weevils and rats. Corn meal, grits, and corn flour are all very nice to have on hand when you are hungry. If you grow less than 100 corn plants in your garden, seed saving will lead to inbred corn that yields less and does poorly. It is better to have at least 100 plants cross-pollinating to save seed. 200 is even better.

Pigeon Peas

Pigeon peas are a staple in Central America, India, and the Caribbean. The plant is a short-lived perennial shrub or small tree that bears an abundance of pods containing small peas in the fall and winter. When we tried them in North Florida they took too long to produce, and the pods froze off too early for eating. If you get a mild winter, they'll produce, but I had a few frosty years in a row and gave up. In the Central to Southern portions of the state, they should give you peas right through winter and into spring. Once they're done producing in spring, you can cut them back and use the greenery to feed and mulch fruit trees and perennials. The pea plants will then grow back and fruit again late in the year.

The woody stems are quite hard and make good cooking fuel for rocket stoves. The peas can be used for shelling when green and the pods are plump, or you can let the pods dry on the branch, and then shell out the dry peas later. Pigeon peas are usually day-length sensitive, which means they will not start blooming until late in the year. Plant the seeds from February through May for fall and winter yields. Pigeon peas produce their own nitrogen and do not generally appreciate being fertilized, though they like good soil, loose ground, and compost.

Plant your pigeon peas in stations 4–6' apart with 2–3 peas in each station (wider spaced pea plants will produce more peas each) rather like you would plant corn in stations. In fact, you can intercrop corn and peas by planting them in stations along with the corn in early spring, adding a couple of peas with your four corn seeds. The corn will produce in 3–4 months, then can be cut down, allowing the pigeon peas to take over the stations and produce a few months later. Plant peas 1–2" deep and water them in. Germination is better if you soak peas overnight before planting.

As a bonus to their edibility, pigeon pea shrubs produce a lot of nitrogen by their roots and biomass above. They can be chopped and dropped to feed your fruit trees, compost pile, or herbivorous animals, and they will grow back again. This is not good for yields however, so do not chop down the peas before they produce for you. In a tropical climate I grew pigeon peas to maturity, harvested them, chopped the pea bushes down to a foot or so high, then had them grow back and produce for me again the next fall and winter. Boil or steam green peas for a few minutes before eating. Dry peas are harder to digest and are best soaked overnight, then boiled until soft or added to stews.

Potatoes

Potatoes are one of the best survival crops in the world, but they are not the easiest to grow in Florida. Though I still grow them, I have found true yams to be much more reliable while being less work. Still, potatoes taste a bit better and make much nicer french fries. Potatoes are a cool-season crop which do not like freezing. Some varieties, like Russet, take too long to produce and will succumb to heat and insects without giving you a good yield. Try to find early varieties for planting—your local hardware store or garden center may sell them as seed potatoes. Potatoes sold as seed are better for planting than grocery store potatoes. Grocery store potatoes may carry diseases. Some of them are also sprayed with sprout inhibitors. Nevertheless, I have grown grocery store potatoes in a pinch and gotten yields from them. I wash them well (without scrubbing, so I do not damage the eyes), then dry them and leave them on a sunny windowsill in fall and winter to start sprouting. If they make good-looking sprouts by planting time, I use them for planting. If they don't, I toss them in the compost.

Loosen the soil deeply before planting potatoes, then make mounded beds about a foot high. They do not like flooded or wet conditions. Add compost, plus a nitrogen and potassium source if you have it. 10-0-10 works well, as do some of the organic amendments I cover in a subsequent chapter. If you grow a crop of peas or beans, then till it under and plant potatoes after it. They like that. Make your potato mounds about three feet apart.

Use potatoes or potato pieces that are about the size of an egg. When you cut up potatoes for seed, try to select decent eyes on them when you do, dividing around the eyes and going for egg-sized pieces. After cutting, let the potato pieces dry out overnight indoors to heal some. They are less likely to rot in the ground that way. Plant potatoes in the ground at about a foot apart, burying them 4" deep. Water deeply when the soil is dry, but do not water too often. Waterlogged soil kills potatoes. As your potatoes grow, watch for fire ants. They are a potato's main enemy in Florida. I put out Amdro in the paths to kill them, as ants love to dig around the base of potatoes and murder the plants. It's infuriating. Kill them all!

As potatoes grow, mound up soil from the paths around their stems to keep the growing tubers from emerging into the sunlight and turning green. After 3–4 months of growth and then blooming, your potatoes will start to die back. Let them die to the ground, then give them a couple weeks before digging up the potatoes beneath. Do not leave your newly-dug potatoes in the sun, as that will cause them to turn green and poisonous. Do not eat green potatoes!

Handle your harvested potatoes carefully and do not wash them if you want them to store longer. Eat the damaged ones first. Store potatoes in a dry, cool, dark location. A basket in the pantry works, as do paper bags. Check them occasionally and remove any that start to rot.

Pumpkins

When a gardener thinks of pumpkins, he probably pictures Halloween decoration rather than a staple food crop. Yet pumpkins and winter squash are quite decent crops in their own right and often taste much better than the flavorless orange pumpkins on sale in October. In Florida, the winning survival staple pumpkin is the native Seminole Pumpkin. Though its origins are murky, it was reported as a native crop by the Spanish back in the 1500s, so if any of us can be called natives, the Seminole pumpkin surely can.

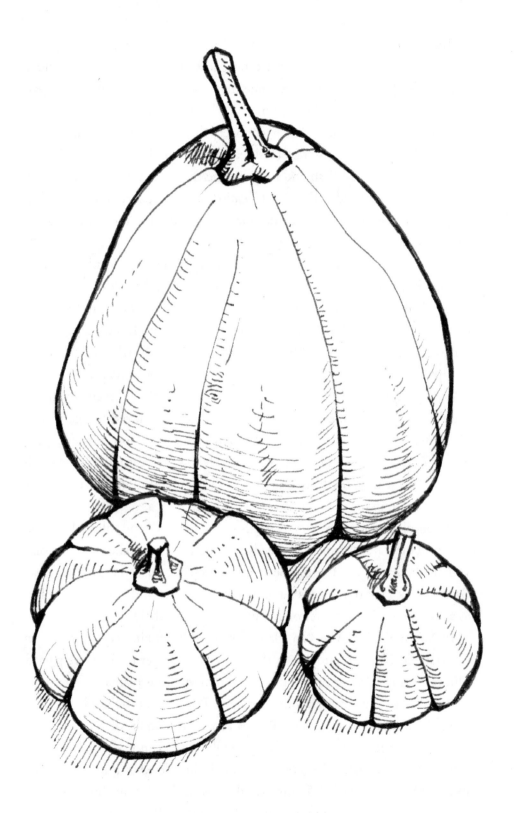

Seminole pumpkins vary greatly in size and shape.

The Seminole pumpkin comes in a wide range of varieties, likely due to crosses. For a couple of years I cataloged strains and growing locations sent to me by readers. There are some that ripen green, though most ripen tan. There are varieties clocking in at 12 lbs or more and others that are only a couple of pounds. What connects them is their rampant growth and reliability, their resistance to diseases and vine borers and their rich orange sweet-flavored flesh and long storage time. Chances are the variety has drifted and crossed with other *C. moschata* species, as it's more of a land race than a true variety, but boy oh boy, it's a good grower and a top-notch survival crop.

It isn't the only pumpkin/winter squash that thrives in Florida, however. There are many varieties of "calabaza" from Central America and Mexico that will take the heat and produce well. There are also varieties from farther north, such as the "Tan Cheese" pumpkin, which produced outrageously for my friend Rick in North/Central Florida. Most Northern varieties of pumpkin suffer in Florida due to powdery mildew, vine borers and the heat, so don't get carried away looking at the gorgeous varieties from cooler climes. Hubbards failed for me in Florida, even though they loved my garden in Tennessee. Boston Marrow is probably a no-go, as are most of the *C. pepo* and *C. Maxima* varieties I tried. Butternut, being a *C. moschata*, can do well in Florida but is regularly eclipsed in production and disease resistance by Seminole Pumpkins. Seminoles just don't quit.

If you plant one pumpkin/winter squash, make it Seminole. Many gardeners in the state save and share seeds. It's good to have friends. If you don't, you might have luck finding Seminole pumpkins in some seed catalogs. Baker Creek Heirloom Seeds has a variety they grow and sell. I avoid eBay as a seed source as there are too many scammers on there.

In South Florida, you can plant Seminole Pumpkins year round. In Central and North Florida, start them after the danger of frost has passed. Direct seeding is better than transplanting for vigorous plants.

Pumpkins need lots of room to roam. They can be trellised, but that is a risky business as pumpkins like to root at the nodes of the vines and gain more strength that way. If they climb, they cannot root all over the place, which also makes them more likely to be murdered by Pumpkin Public Enemy #1, the vine borer. A pumpkin that gets drilled by vine borers but has a lot of rooted sections will shrug off the damage and keep going. Sometimes the damaged vines will even end up divided into two separate plants that will both go on to produce pumpkins. The modular nature of *C. moschata* pumpkins really helps them cope with the stress of Florida growing.

Plant pumpkins on mounds that are 8' apart in all directions. You can probably push them as close as 5', but don't go any closer than that as crowding will reduce yields. Put them in full sun. They'll take half, but tend to run for the light if they get the chance and will be weak in shade. The vines can grow a surprisingly long distance and will fight for space and reduce yields if you crowd them. Currently I grow pumpkins along the edge of my garden where they can ramble down into the drainage ditch and around the back of my compost pile and under my starfruit tree, which keeps them from running wild all over my tomatoes and pak choi.

I grow pumpkins on mounds, like most everyone, because that's just the

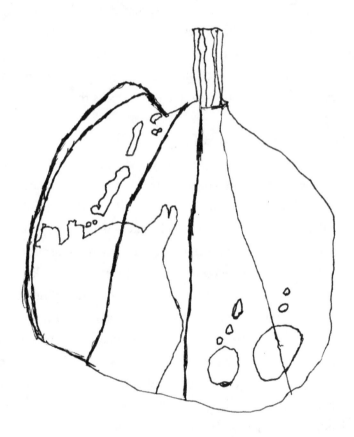

Various tropical pumpkins, including Central American calabazas, grow well in Florida. (Drawing by my 8-year-old son.)

way everybody does it. Where I change the game is by burying a bunch of nitrogenous material under the mound. I call it the "Melon Pit" method, because it's also great for growing melons.

To make melon pits, dig a hole that's at least 2' deep. 3' is better. This is easy in sand but hard in clay or on lime rock soils. Do your best. Now throw in some kitchen scraps and other horrid stinky things. Meat or fish scraps are great. Dog droppings are fine. Humanure, goat organs, an old lasagna, raw chicken manure, hair, a shovel of compost, a dead pet, your enemies, whatever. We grew a great Seminole Pumpkin over a dead rat once. The idea is to put some super rich food underneath the vines that the roots will find and kick-start the plant's growth. This will not hurt you—no one will know what you did, and it won't make you sick. Once you've thrown a horrifying thing or three into melon pit, cover it over and make a mound on top. Make sure your loathsome, wretched, vomit-inducing, nasty, horrible material is a solid 2–3' down if you can, as that usually keeps roving critters from digging it up again. Now plant 3–5 pumpkin seeds in the mound around an inch deep and water deeply. In 4–8 days, they should pop up. Within a week or two, their roots will go deep enough to hit the scary stuff and they'll turn deep green. In a couple more weeks they start running and you are off to the races.

Keep the weeds and grass down at first so your pumpkins can conquer the space without competition. Once they really get rolling, you won't have to worry about weeding as the vines will cover everything. Water as needed. It's normal for pumpkins to wilt in the mid-day heat, so don't worry too much about that, but if you get up early in the morning and your pumpkins are wilting, you either need to water or look for vine borer damage. Vine borers are nasty insects that lay their eggs in the stem of pumpkin vines. The eggs hatch and turn into worms that chew their way along inside the stems, causing your plants to lose their connection to water. As I mentioned above, Seminole pumpkins can often shrug off the damage due to their ability to root at the nodes, but I've still lost them on occasion. When I attempted to grow the much more susceptible Hubbard squash, I dusted the vine bases every week with Sevin dust to keep the borers out. With Seminole pumpkins, however, I skip the evil pesticides and just let them root everywhere. If you move the end of pumpkin vines that are more than a few days old, you'll see that the nodes on the new growth are already starting to put out roots. I encourage this by throwing handfuls of sand and mulch over nodes in the vines, figuring that more roots equals a much higher chance for the plant to survive the inevitable borer attacks.

If white mildew shows up on your pumpkin leaves, try treating it with a few tablespoons of plain yogurt shaken up into a spray bottle of rain or well water (chlorinated water kills the bacteria in yogurt!) and sprayed on the leaves in the evening. The beneficial bacteria in the yogurt seem to beat the infection down. Generally, I only have mildew appearing on my vines late in the season when they're about to die anyhow so I don't worry about it.

Many people have written me with variations of "Help! My pumpkins are blooming, but they aren't setting fruit!" This is normal for members of the squash family. First, you'll get a bunch of blooms that are just males, producing pollen but lacking an ovary. Later, as the plant matures, it will start producing the occasional female bloom. These are identifiable by looking at the base of the flower. It will have what looks like a small pumpkin beneath the bloom—the ovary—unlike the male blooms which are just a yellow funnel with no bulge at the bottom. If female flowers are fertilized by a bee or other insect, or by the gardener, the nascent pumpkin at the bottom will usually start to grow into an actual pumpkin. If you aren't seeing a lot of bee activity, just go out with a paintbrush and dust the brush around on the anthers (the part where you see the pollen grains) of a male flower, then dust it on the stigma (it's the center piece coming up from inside the bloom) of a female flower. Good job—you are now a human bee-ing. Buzz buzz.

Sometimes pollination doesn't take, and the bloom will drop off. This may be because the vine is young or because weather conditions were not right or because the female bloom failed to meet the male bloom of her dreams. Don't worry about it. The plant will make more blooms. If your vines grow smaller and weaker as they move away from the melon pit, I recommend watering them with a foliar fertilizer. Diluted urine works really well on them, as does Dave's Fetid Swamp Water, as do various commercial fertilizers. Make sure they get some water now and again so they can maintain their rampant growth. Pumpkin vines will climb over anything and everything, often growing a foot or more in a day. I've seen pumpkins hanging out of trees before. If they start to invade your garden beds, gently pick up the new vines and turn them in another direction. Sometimes I turn them in a curving 90 degrees and stick a stick in the ground next to the vine to keep it there. Steve Solomon sometimes chops the ends off, but he's more ornery than I am, so I stick to being a namby-pamby vine whisperer just in case I cut down on their potential yields.

Once you have fertilized flowers, the pumpkins drop their yellow bloom and begin to swell. They start out a pale green color and mature to their final colors over a month or so. A pumpkin or winter squash is ready to harvest when the stem yellows or browns or the main vine dies. You'll be tempted to cook one right away, but the flavor of a newly harvested pumpkin pales in comparison to one that has been allowed to sit on the shelf and cure for a month or more. That's when the sweetness and flavor really develops inside. It's wonderful to see a row of pumpkins sitting on a shelf as well. Seminoles can keep for quite a long time. The smaller ones with the darker tan skin seem to keep longer than the larger ones with paler tan skin, but I have had both sitting at room temperature inside for over a year without spoiling. One small one I was given by Jacksonville Permaculture Guru Alex Ojeda kept for two years before we opened it up and ate it. It was rather dry inside but still sweet and edible. What a great survival crop! My guess is that the Indians inadvertently bred this variety for storage by eating their pumpkins through the year and saving the last ones for seed, though that's just conjecture on my part.

Pumpkins can be added to soups, cut in half with the seed mass scooped out and roasted in the oven or baked into delicious pies. The taste of a Seminole pumpkin is much like that of a good orange sweet potato, rich and buttery. The seeds can also be roasted or fried in oil for a delicious snack. Just be sure to save some for next year. Seed saving is simple. Just scoop some out and dry them on paper towels for a week or so, then pop them into a sealed baggie or jar to store in the fridge until you need them. They'll still germinate after a couple of years if kept this way. They do not store as well at room temperature, lasting perhaps a year before losing viability. Just be sure to label what you have. I currently have a mess of unlabeled baggies of seeds that I thought I would remember but don't. My current hills have quite a few different types in them, probably including acorns and butternuts and Seminole crosses and calabazas. *C. moschata* types regularly cross with others inside the species, which means if you grow a long-necked Central American pumpkin next to your Seminoles, then save seed, you may end up with weird, long-necked Seminole types the next year.

As a final note on Seminoles: they do not like the high heat and bugs of midsummer in Florida. Get them in early. One year I had them pop up in my compost heap and run rampant, then die back in July and August, then somewhat recover in the fall and bear me a second crop. This is not common, however, so plant accordingly.

Sunflowers

Sunflowers are a Native American staple crop now commonly grown as an ornamental or bird food. It's still a decent survival crop with oil-rich seeds which are good raw or roasted. Plant large varieties of sunflower a few feet apart in amended soil and water well as they get established. They transplant quite well if you start them in flats or you can direct sow into your garden. The heads are prone to being eaten by bugs and birds in Florida so I do not count on them as a main crop, but they are worth trying. Harvest the sunflower heads when the petals have all dropped, and the main stem around the head is yellowing, then hang them to dry somewhere where they won't get devoured. In a pinch, you can plant the sunflower seeds from a birdseed or squirrel food mix and get decent sunflowers.

Sweet Potatoes

Sweet potatoes are a top-notch staple calorie crop in the Sunshine State. Sweet potato beds are planted by cutting vines from existing sweet potatoes and planting them out. These are called "slips". I plant sweet potato slips about 12–16" apart in rows 2–3' apart. Loosen the ground before you plant them to ensure they can make decent roots. Sweet potatoes prefer sand to clay soils and need space to expand beneath the soil. If you are on limerock soils or gardening on a parking lot, give them a good foot and a half of decent soil by making raised mounds or beds or using containers. Slips do not need to be rooted before you plant them. Just cut pieces of sweet potato stem, remove all the leaves except for one or just the little ones, then plant them on their sides a couple inches deep with one end of the slip sticking out of the ground, then water them. For a few days, they'll wilt and look awful, but they root readily and start running quickly. At the base of each planted slip, potatoes will form in a few months.

If you do not have slips to plant, it is easy to start your own from begged, borrowed, or purchased sweet potato roots. I once bought an assortment of different sweet potatoes in varying colors from an organic market, started slips, then planted them willy-nilly in my garden. That year we had a lot of fun digging potatoes that ranged from white to yellow to orange and deep purple. To start slips from sweet potato roots, lay them on their sides in soil just beneath the surface. Water regularly, but don't make them sopping wet. Keep this flat in half-sun. In a few weeks, shoots will start emerging from the roots. As they grow to 12" long, you can carefully trim or break them off to plant out. Planting season for sweet potatoes is year-round in South Florida and after all danger of frost in Central and North Florida. You can keep planting there until June or so, then the heat makes it hard to establish a bed except in cooler areas or in beds of mulch. Sweet potatoes will grow in mulch or bare ground, but they do not like full shade. Dappled shade will still get you some potatoes and I had good luck planting them in mulched areas of my food forest in North Florida, where they bore quite well. It's best to plant in different areas from year to year, but you might get away with growing them a couple of years in the same spot. My potato yields decreased greatly when I just let the vines keep running and running for a couple of years.

Sweet potatoes like organic matter in the ground and really appreciate potassium (wood ashes are a good source), but do not feed them much—if

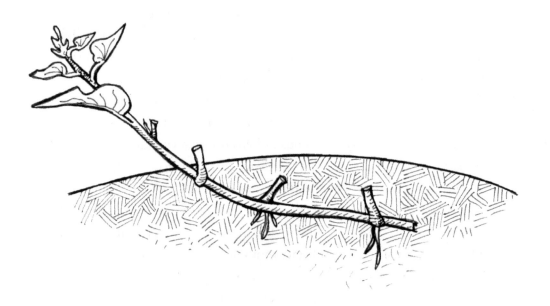

A well-planted sweet potato slip roots rapidly.

any—nitrogen or they will produce abundant vines and few roots. I have made this mistake before. The plants looked amazing but made almost no roots whatsoever.

Sweet potato leaves are edible raw or cooked but are reportedly much better for you cooked as they contain some anti-nutrients when raw.

After a few months in the ground, you can do some digging to see if your plants are making roots. The boniato types I have grown—that is, mostly white varieties from Latin America and the Caribbean—took much longer to produce than the traditional American orange types. White varieties are starchier and drier and not as sweet but make a nice change from the very sweet orange types.

Sweet potato roots can be boiled or fried and, like the leaves, are not good to eat raw.

When you harvest your sweet potatoes, give them a week or two to lay out and cure in a shady, dry location or they will not taste as nice and sweet as the ones you buy from the store. Do not wash them before curing and be careful not to damage roots when you dig them or they won't keep as long. Once they are mature in the ground, you can dig them as you like over the course of some months or just harvest them all, cure them, and let them sit in a cool, dry location in cardboard boxes or baskets. I had them keep in my air-conditioned pantry for months. Remove any potatoes that go bad and eat damaged ones first.

Turnips

Turnips are a cool-season crop that was a traditional staple food in Europe. They are not the best things to eat, but they can keep you alive in a pinch. Direct seed them in the garden when it is still cold or cool outside and long before the heat of summer. They will not keep growing in the heat. In North Florida we planted them in November and then again in February, often by sprinkling a packet of them over an area of loosened soil and lightly covering the little seeds. Do not plant too deeply. Just a quarter inch or so is fine, and keep them well watered until they sprout and develop their first true leaves. Turnips need some space, so thin out any that are closer than 6" from each other in a bed. Eat the thinnings—they are good. In fact, we like turnip greens much more than the roots. Turnips will give you a harvest in two months or so if they are happy, fattening rapidly in decent soil with regular water. Thin progressively as they get bigger and you can start eating the 1" roots and keep going with the wider and wider spaced roots until you eat the last few 3–4" diameter roots. When the heat arrives, harvest and store the rest, chopping off the tops and putting them in the crisper drawer of your fridge. Otherwise, they will bolt and put up a seed stalk or just die in the sun. In South Florida, you can plant turnips from October through January for regular harvests.

Yams

As everyone knows by this point, I am a huge fan of true yams, also known as "name" yams (pronounced "nah-may"). They are not related even distantly to sweet potatoes despite sharing the name "yam". Yams are a climbing vine that can make huge roots beneath the ground. So far, I have grown purple, white, and yellow greater yams (*Dioscorea alata*), potato yams (*Dioscorea escuelenta)*, Chinese yams, also known as cinnamon vine (*Dioscorea polystachya*), the edible variety of *D. bulbifera*, which bears potato-sized roots on hanging vines and is quite rare, Lisbon yams (an improved *D. alata* cultivar) and a few other types I can't find the names for. My favorite producers are the white/yellow *D. alata* types, also known as the "greater yam" or the "winged yam". It's on the Florida invasive species list which tells you just how easy a crop it is to grow. In the Caribbean and tropical portions of Asia, Central America and Africa, yams are staple crops that feed everyone through the fall and winter months and on into spring. On some islands, they grow rampantly in the wild and are dug with machetes by the poor during the winter dry season. In Florida, finding propagative material can be a wild goose chase, but it is by no means impossible. I have seen "name" yams for sale at Publix and if you buy one of them, you can divide it and plant multiple hills of yams. There are also quite a few edible yams growing wild in the state; however, make sure you do not mistake the common air potato (*Dioscorea bulbifera*) for the edible *Dioscorea alata*. The wild specimens of *D. bulbifera* in Florida are not edible and are poisonous. *D. alata*, however, can be found in the wild and propagated provided you can tell it apart from its poisonous cousin. You'll find a comparative illustration in the section on wild plant foraging. You can also look up my yam/air potato identification video on YouTube to see the difference in growth and leaves and you'll be an expert in no time.

Yams can be propagated by a variety of means. You can take existing roots, like the one you found at an ethnic produce market, and cut it into pieces about half the size of your fist, making sure you keep as much of the skin intact on each piece as possible, then dust the cut portions of the individual pieces with ashes to prevent rot and fungi, then plant them in the ground or in a pot to sprout, then transplant those sprouted pieces into the ground later.

I have also started *D. alata* from cuttings, but did not get to compare the yields to tuber-grown and I am sure they will not produce as large a root in the first year. One of the best ways to grow most yams is from the small, bulbous, aerial roots that grow on the vines in fall. These are called bulbils. As the yam vines die back in fall and winter, they fall to the ground and sprout in the spring.

Yams can be planted from fall through spring no matter where you are in the state. They have a pronounced dormancy period that lasts from November until some time in the spring, earlier or later depending on the species and rainfall. Yams like compost and mulch at planting but don't seem to need much else. And they don't even need that. Plant your yams

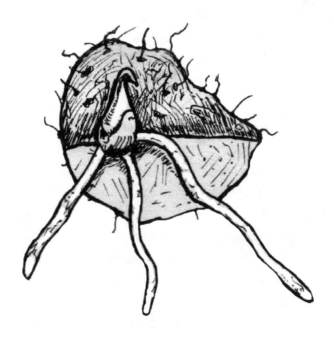

Cut pieces of yam create shoots and roots at the end of their dormant season.

about 2' apart in rows 4' apart, or make individual hills 2–3' apart. Plant cut pieces, bulbils or sprouted pieces 2–4" inches deep so they don't dry out in the ground. It's important to make sure you plant in a spot with loose soil so the roots can expand down. Hills aren't a bad idea because they're easier to dig later, though they dry out faster than flat-planting. Make sure you have a trellis in mind before the vines start growing out of control. When they come up, they shoot up very fast, probably growing a foot a day or more, and will turn into a tangled mess if you aren't ready for them. I like to hammer rebar in the ground and run a rope across the top and strings down, as I do for pole beans. Individual stakes work well, but try to keep them 6' or so tall above the ground. Branches with some side twigs left on work well. Cattle or hog panels or a fence also work well. I have also had good luck letting them climb along fences and up into trees. It may be shady under a tree, but they'll climb up into the canopy quickly and unfurl an abundance of leaves at the top, capturing the sunlight they need to grow their tubers. I once pollarded a sweetgum sapling at about 7' tall and planted a few yams around the base every year to climb it, throwing the cut sweetgum leaves and branches on the ground as mulch for the yams. At the end of the year when we dug yams, I cut off the top of the tree again. This worked well for years. If you have a wide-spreading tree, you can plant yams under it and run strings down from the branches and let them climb up into it. I do not recommend covering all your favorite fruit trees with yams (though I still plant a few), but I view all magnolias, oaks, dogwoods, and other non-food trees to be fair game as living yam trellises.

When the vines die back in fall and winter, you can dig yams or leave them in the ground until you want them. They usually run from 3–10 lbs in size the first year, depending on how well they were treated, how much rain they got, and how fertile the soil is. If you wait too long to dig them, they'll start sprouting again in the spring. You can dig them when the vines first appear, but don't wait more than a couple weeks as the roots will start deteriorating as they feed the vines. If you want to grow really big yams or don't need the food at the time of resprouting, just let the vines go. They'll suck the energy out of the yam in the ground and it will shrink and rot away as it feeds the new aboveground growth. The second year growth on well-rooted yams is incredible. I've seen a fat vine shoot up eight feet from a large root without putting out a single leaf, reaching for the sky and sunlight as fast as it could grow. These vines will be bigger and make more leaves than they did in the first year. Over summer and fall they'll build a new and larger root beneath the ground. Second-year yam tubers can easily surpass 20 lbs.

Once you have yams, it's easy to grow more. You'll get a few bulbils for planting from first-year yams and a bunch from second-year ones. So long as you don't dig them they just keep growing every year, though parts of the roots will get gnarled and woody. One really cool thing about yams is that you can harvest them in fall, then cut off the top couple of inches of the root where the vine had been, then plant it back into the hole where you dug the yam. This top part is called the "head" and can be planted over and over again and it will grow new vines and a root beneath it. If you want to keep already dug yams over the winter, just put a bunch in a bucket somewhere and throw some leaves or sawdust or a bit of soil over them until you want to plant them again in spring. Freezing weather kills the above-ground growth of yams, but that happens late enough in the year that it won't affect your yields. Furthermore, new growth on yams invariably shows up after the last frost date in Florida so you do not have to worry about them getting frozen.

Yams contain oxalate acid crystals in the roots so they cannot be eaten raw. Some people's skin is irritated by peeling yams so wear gloves when you process them. Just cut off the top couple of woody inches—the head—and then peel the rest of the yam. It's slippery and slimy when raw so be careful not to slip and cut yourself as you peel. Then chop the peeled roots into pieces and use them as you would white potatoes, cooking until they are fork tender. This usually takes about twenty minutes of boiling. They are good in stews or boiled and mashed. Yams also cook quite well in a crockpot. Mashed yams with cheese, butter and salt are excellent. If you cut yams into smaller pieces and boil them until they are soft, you can then pour off the water and fry them into yam fries. The flavor of most yams is similar to a white potato, starchy and not sweet. If you make beef stew and substitute yams for potatoes your guests won't even know the difference. Though slimy when raw, they are not at all slimy when cooked, so fear not. This is just a great staple carbohydrate crop. I am eternally grateful to my friend Craig Hepworth for sharing his love of yams for me years ago, when he told me how he thought it was the top survival staple crop to grow in Florida. After my first year of growing them, I found myself in complete agreement.

If I had to pick one staple survival crop for Florida, yams would be it.

Chapter 3

NUTRITION CROPS FOR FLORIDA

Once you've put in your staple crops, it's time to think about greens for nutrition and bulking up meals. Living on boiled cassava and corn without greens is a good way to end up with nutritional deficiencies, not to mention boring dinners. We'll start with the best nutrition-rich easy-to-grow Florida vegetables, then I'll cover a few additional crops you might want to add.

Amaranth

Amaranth is an old staple crop that is grown as a grain and as a vegetable. It is time-consuming as a grain but easy as a green. Think of amaranth like a warm-season spinach that gives you lots of greens and can be cut repeatedly. Raw, the leaves are high in oxalic acid so I do not recommend eating them unless stir-fried, steamed, or boiled.

Amaranth grows in heat and drought and often re-seeds. It likes open areas and broken ground, which is why weedy versions of it regularly appear in tilled fields. The much-hated pigweed that plagues hay farmers and gardeners is a form of amaranth and its leaves are just as edible as cultivated amaranth, though they are much smaller. Cultivated amaranth comes in two main forms: grain and vegetable. The former produces massive seed heads, often in beautiful colors. The latter produces large leaves, which also come in a rainbow of colors. We are currently growing "tiger amaranth", which has large red and green leaves, as well as another local green type with spotted leaves. We have also grown "golden amaranth", which has large leaves and large golden-yellow seed heads. That was a gorgeous plant.

Amaranth can be planted year-round in South Florida and after danger of frost in Central and North Florida. The seeds are tiny and are hard to plant with precision so I usually just loosen up some soil and scatter them, then throw a dusting of soil over the area. Do not plant them too deep. If you need more control, plant them in trays or a flat of potting soil by sprinkling, then let them grow a little and transplant them into rows. They take crowding pretty well but will spread out and produce better leaves if you give them a foot or two in between plants. Pick individual leaves as the plants grow or just chop the tops off and cook them, stems and all, when the stems are still young and tender. Plants will grow back beneath where you cut as long as you don't cut too low on the stems. I usually cut off the top six inches or so, which induces branching and more shoots which I can do the same with a couple weeks later.

You can start harvesting amaranth about a month after planting. It grows fast and will keep you in greens for a couple of months before it decides it wants to flower. Then the leaves get a lot thinner and energy goes into shooting up blooms. Just let them bloom when the leaf production drops off, then you can harvest the seeds. The bloom heads are full of flower chaff that releases tiny seeds when it starts drying up. Go to dry heads and gently rub them between your palms to make the seeds fall into a container. A lot of dried flower heads will fall in as well, but you can blow on them gently and spin the seeds around in a bowl to separate the seeds from the chaff. Or you can just let the whole mess of seeds and chaff dry on your counter for a few days, then bag it all and put it in the fridge until you're ready to scatter seeds, chaff, and all onto a new amaranth bed.

Amaranth's cousin *Celosia*, also known as quail grass, can be grown and eaten the same way but has the additional benefit of very pretty pink and white fox-tail blooms. It is a little weaker on leaf production but looks great both in the garden and the landscape.

Beans
See notes on production above in the calorie crop section.

Cabbage
Cabbage grows well during the fall, winter and early spring but cannot take the summer heat. In North Florida, plant cabbage in early November for fall gardens and in February for spring gardens. South Floridians can plant cabbage any time from October through February. Cabbages are quite nutrient dense and high in vitamin C, especially when made into sauerkraut.

Though a little trickier to grow than the other vegetables on this list, they are well worth the effort.

I have both direct-seeded and grown cabbages from transplants. I find the latter to work better, and it's easy to start your own transplants. Cabbages like a good bit of nutrition in the soil before planting. If you can get a decent nitrogen source—like blood meal, composted chicken manure, compost, alfalfa meal or pellets, or compost—and add it to the bed before planting cabbage, it will help a lot. I also throw down handfuls of ashes, kelp meal and bone meal if I have it. Or mix a couple of cups of 10-10-10 into each 4' x 8' bed before planting, mixing it in well so you don't burn the new plants.

Plant seeds or transplants 16–24" apart in rows 2–3' apart. Cabbage likes full sun but only in the cool time of the year. You can get away with half-sun, especially if they get morning sun. Cabbages like mulching but will grow in bare soil as well.

Keep them well-watered and they grow quickly. For a while, they have an open form and just about the time you start saying, "Hey, are these things EVER gonna make heads?", they start to make heads. I harvest heads when the center is about the size of a grapefruit. There are larger cabbage types, but I do not think they are well-suited to Florida as they take too long to get going. Try to get cabbages that resist splitting, as that can be a problem. Though it's a resource-intensive way to garden, I once took Dewitt Sunbelt woven landscape fabric from my plant nursery stock and burned holes into it with a tin can heated on a torch, putting the holes right at cabbage spacing. Then I laid it down over a newly dug bed and planted my cabbages in the holes to keep them weed-free. They grew wonderfully and seemed to appreciate the mulch, despite it being made of evil plastic and totally non-organic. Cabbages do not do well with competition.

When the heat of summer comes, make sure you don't leave your cabbages in the ground as they will burn and split and rot quickly. Cabbages take about three months to make good heads so plant them early. If you want to start your own from seeds, Johnny's Selected Seeds' "Storage #4" is a great hybrid type that does well in Florida. I have also had luck with every type I bought from the local hardware store transplant rack.

I like to grow a lot of cabbage for two reasons. One, I have a large family and they all like cabbage. Two, Rachel makes awesome sauerkraut which keeps for months in the fridge.

How to Make Homemade Sauerkraut

by Rachel the Good

As with most of my recipes, creative expression is the name of the game. After all, it's easy to buy exactly the amount of veggies and fruits you need for a recipe from the grocery store. However, when you're talking about cooking what you've grown, you will often find that your garden isn't reading the same cookbook you are and doesn't want to cooperate. This recipe is very versatile.

I use a half gallon mason jar, which pretty much holds two cabbages worth of sauerkraut, but feel free to scale it up or down. You can include other veggies into the mix, or even leave out the cabbage all together. Green beans, carrots, broccoli, and cucumbers work well, just to name a few. Regarding brine strength: the ratio is anywhere from 1–4 tablespoons of salt per qt. of water. That's a big range! Experimentation on your part is necessary. For cabbage, I usually use 1 tablespoon per cup of water. For thicker veggies, I will increase the salt to 2 or 3 tablespoons per cup Also, most fermenting recipes will advise against using iodized salt. They say it alters the flavor or color of the finished product, I can't remember which. Personally I haven't noticed a difference and, since the ferment will still work, I aways use whatever type of salt I have on hand.

Ingredients:

- 2 heads of cabbage
- Garlic cloves, peeled (optional)
- Salt
- Water

If you are using garlic, add a clove or two to the bottom of a half-gallon mason jar. Cut heads of cabbage into fourths and remove the core. Then slice the cabbages, starting from the pointy end of each quarter. Stuff the sliced cabbage into the jar. If you want more garlic, add some when your jar is half full. Keep stuffing in cabbage until it reaches the neck of the jar. You can add even more garlic on the top if you want.

Dissolve 2 tablespoons of salt into 2 cups of water and pour into the jar over the cabbage and garlic. You will need at lease this much brine, and probably more. Mix up more if you need it and pour over the cabbage and garlic until your brine reaches the highest thread on the jar. Screw on the lid tightly and give the jar a good shake to get the brine into all the crevices. Open the lid again and add more brine until it is level with the highest thread again. Save any leftover brine in a covered container on the counter for topping off later.

Set the jar on the counter, in a place where you will easily see it, on top of a plate, with the jar slightly loosened. Three times a day, tighten the lid and give it a good shake, place it back onto the plate, and loosen the lid again. As it starts to ferment, some of the brine will probably overflow from the jar, so add more if you need to.

After 24 hours, your ferment is in full swing, but your sauerkraut will need more time to really get some good flavors going. How much time is up to you. In our climate—without air conditioning—it usually takes 3 days. Taste it every day and when it is tart enough for your liking, put it into the refrigerator. At this point you no longer need to shake it or add more brine. Sauerkraut keeps for months.

Enjoy!

Cabbage is good raw or cooked, in coleslaw, chopped and sautéed with scrambled eggs, as stuffed leaves, or in soups and stews. Fermentation greatly increases the available vitamin C in cabbage as well as healing your gut and building a healthy digestive system.

Saving seed on cabbages is best left to the experts as it is a complicated process and I am not sure how possible it is in Florida due to our hot climate.

Chaya

Chaya is another one of those plants that people complain is hard to find. Once you find it, though, you'll be glad you have it. Various people around the state have it and it is propagated by stem cuttings. Ask around and make friends with local gardeners, particularly permaculture enthusiasts. You'll find some, then you'll have it to share with others. Also known as Mexican tree spinach, chaya is a perennial shrub or small tree that produces a massive amount of nutrient-dense leaves. It tolerates wet and dry weather, and the pests leave it alone. There are two main types of chaya in Florida; one that seems to be a wilder form with jagged leaves that is sometimes grown to

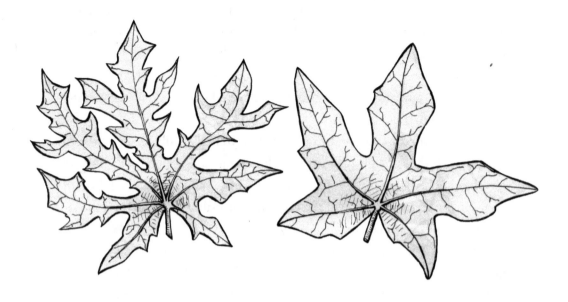

The jagged-leafed wilder form of chaya on left, the better eating type on right.

attract butterflies, and a second variety with roughly maple-shaped leaves that is better for eating. I prefer the latter but grow both.

I plant chaya outside my main garden beds, along the edges of my property, in my food forest, in bad areas of ground and wherever I feel like sticking in a cutting. You literally just need to cut off a 12–16" piece of stem from a bush, then let it sit out in the shade for a day so the sap at the end can dry, then dig a little hole and stick it in the ground half-way. Water it if the ground is really dry. If you're getting rain, you don't even have to bother. I left some cuttings on the ground and forgot about them and they grew without even being buried. This stuff is almost like a cactus. Chaya grows quite big if you let it so don't crowd them. 4–5' between plants is good, and remember it is a perennial so wherever you stick it, you'll have it for a long, long time. It's not at all invasive, either, and is easy to chop down and dig up if you tire of it in a certain location.

Plant chaya during the warm months so it roots well. Plants like full sun and get spindly and weak in the shade. In Central and North Florida the plants are sometimes killed back by frosts but regrow in spring. The first year after planting, chaya often grows slowly. In the second year it usually leaps and produces a large amount of edible leaves. Cutting it back will stimulate the growth of more leaves and stems. It will get leggy otherwise and can get out of reach.

Chaya leaves are toxic raw. Boil leaves and young shoots in water for twenty minutes and they will off-gas their cyanide compounds and become safe to eat. Younger leaves are better to eat than older ones, as the older leaves can get papery and tough. Do not cook chaya in aluminum pots as they are reported to react poorly with aluminum and may cause digestive upset.

I know, cyanide and digestive upset don't sound good, but trust me: cooked chaya is one of the best greens you can get, and this is hands-down the easiest green you can grow in Florida.

Collards

Think of collards like an easier-to-grow version of cabbage and plant them the same way. They are care-free and produce abundantly. Boiled collards with pepper vinegar is a Southern staple. Don't miss out on it.

Kale

Kale is one of those superfoods we're all supposed to eat, like blueberries, garlic, and Dollar Store Cheese Puffs.

Scratch that. Blueberries are overrated.

Kale is a cool-season vegetable that likes moderately decent soil and some water. Plant kale 12" apart in rows 2' apart for good production. They like mulch and compost, as well as nitrogen. Composted chicken manure or cottonseed meal will grow nice kale, though they also grow well on homemade compost. Plant kale from November through February in Florida. It's easy to grow from seed or transplants. You can just overseed a little, then thin and eat the small kale until they reach your desired spacing. I tried growing "tree kale" in Florida, but it did not perform as well as advertised, so I just stick to the boring seed-rack kales now.

Kale can be eaten raw or cooked and is quite good sautéed with scrambled eggs and bacon for breakfast.

Longevity Spinach

Longevity spinach (*Gynura procumbens*) was made for Florida. It's so easy to grow and healthy that you'll wonder how you went without it. The leaves have an interesting fresh flavor that I immediately liked. It's a good salad stuffer or a cooked green.

*Longevity spinach (*Gynura procumbens*) is an excellent perennial green for Florida.*

Longevity spinach is a half-vining herbaceous perennial that tolerates poor soil, drought and heat but benefits from water and compost. Propagation is by stem cuttings. Just break off a piece of stem, stick it in the ground, water it, and it will root. Longevity spinach takes sun and shade well. Okinawa spinach, its pretty purple-and-green cousin, has a milder flavor but was much less hardy in my North Florida garden, wilting in the heat and dying in the winters.

Longevity spinach does not like frost and often dies if it freezes to the ground. If a frost is coming, take a few cuttings from your plants in fall and put them in a pot to root, then plant them out again in spring.

Finding longevity spinach may not be easy. Ask around and make friends. People are often trading plants in the comments of my YouTube videos, so be friendly and you'll soon find yourself with some cuttings—and once you have them, you're off to the longevity spinach races.

Malabar Spinach

Malabar spinach is another exotic tropical green that does well in Florida. Its leaves can grow large and are fleshy and mucilaginous. Some eat them raw, but I find they make my throat feel scratchy unless they are cooked. On Caribbean islands, Malabar spinach can be seen rambling over fences and rum shacks, down the sides of houses, and on stick trellises in garden beds. It's a perennial with tender climbing vines that comes in two main varieties, green and red. Both taste the same to me.

Malabar spinach likes sun, water and decent soil. At various times of

Malabar spinach is a beautiful climbing vine with fleshy leaves.

the year it will bloom and drop small purple fruit to the ground which later sprout to make new vines. It's easy to grow from transplants, but seed germination isn't as easy. For some reason, they seem to grow better when they plant themselves than when planted on purpose.

Cut pieces of stem and stick them in moist soil and they root readily. Give Malabar spinach a place to climb and it will ramble all over. In North Florida it will usually get killed in the winter by cold, as it's a truly tropical plant. However, the seeds of summer often sprout again and give you vines the next year. In South Florida, Malabar spinach is a year-round crop.

Add leaves to stews and stir-fries. You can also make them really unhealthy by taking an egg, a few cups of flour and water, plus some salt and garlic powder, then smashing Malabar spinach leaves into it to make a Malabar spinach dough. Fry patties in oil to make delicious fried Malabar spinach cakes.

Moringa

Moringa, "the Miracle Tree", is touted as a cure-all and has now been planted in yards all over Florida.

Moringa is a fast-growing tropical tree species with multiple uses. In its native range, the tree's large pods are picked young and served as a delicious vegetable comparable to asparagus. Unfortunately, gaining consistent pod yields in Florida isn't easy, so here the moringa is often grown for its tiny leaves. Because of the tree's remarkably ability to mine the ground for nutrients, the leaves are loaded with nutrition—and even contain complete protein, a relative rarity in the Vegetable Kingdom. There are claims that the tree is also medicinal, killing fungal infections, fighting cancer, giving you the ability to fly, etc. I'm not sure about all those bits and pieces, but its nutrition has been proven in the lab and on the ground in Africa, where dried leaves are used as a powerful antidote to malnutrition in infants and nursing mothers.

Beyond those benefits, moringa also grows at a ridiculous rate. The first time I planted seeds, the trees shot towards the sky at an astounding speed, reaching 20' before winter frosts knocked them back to the ground. This rate of growth means you'll have plenty of leaves to harvest. Bonus: moringa leaves are excellent livestock feed. The tree is also good for chopping up and adding to compost piles, since its soft wood deteriorates rapidly. I've also dried the thin leaves in my greenhouse and then crushed them into powder.

I then sprinkle that dust over newly prepared garden beds for a little extra dose of fertilization. Moringa seems to give young plants a kick.

In South Florida Moringa grows year-round without protection, but in Central and North Florida, it stalls in winter. The trees cannot stand frost, and the entire tree—including the thinner trunks—will turn into soppy mush if it gets much below 32 degrees, though the tree usually resprouts from the ground once the weather warms up in spring. I had a friend who planted some moringa trees, lost them all in a brutal freeze, then figured they were dead and started pulling them up in the spring—until she noticed tiny shoots rising from the ground where one of the young trees had been. These trees are tough! They don't always come back, but they usually do. North Floridians suffer through occasional freezes down into the teens which is way too cold for the above-ground growth of a moringa tree. To give my trees a head start on next year, and to increase leaf yield, I coppice my moringas at about 3' tall in the late fall before the first frost. I then put a 2' diameter ring of 4' tall chicken wire around the trunk, stake it in, then stuff the ring full of leaves, pine needles, straw, or all three. Sometimes I'll also throw a blanket or tarp on top of that for even more frost protection. This method keeps the main above-ground trunk from getting whacked by frost. When the tree comes back in spring, it beats the living daylights out of the ones that weren't protected.

Moringa is propagated from seeds and cuttings, though the first method gives you much stronger plants. Cuttings sometimes take easily—and sometimes don't. If you want to give cuttings a try, lop off a branch ranging in diameter from 1–2" and at least 2' long and bury the bottom third in the ground. It usually starts sprouting new growth in a few weeks—or it decides to rot. I might use cuttings for an instant barrier fence, but seeding moringa trees can reach 20' tall in their first year so I usually just grow those.

Beyond being good fertilizer and livestock fodder, moringa leaves are nice added to soups, salads, stir-fries, and eggs. Snapping the large, compound leaves off the tree is easy, and once you do that, you can strip the little leaflets off into whatever you're cooking. If you expect freezing weather, strip all the leaves from the trees and spread them out to dry indoors on a tarp, then you'll still have them to add to soups or to make tea from. This plant is a nutritional powerhouse. A little moringa each day keeps the doctor away.

Mustard

When you think of mustard, you probably think of a tangy, bright-yellow condiment used almost exclusively on hot dogs, hamburgers, and pretzels.

I love the inexpensive yellow mustard I grew up with as a kid, though my wife has more class and likes grainier, brown, spicy mustards in fancy containers.

Either way, when most of us think of mustard, we think of the condiment made from the plant's seeds, not the mustard plant itself.

Yet mustard greens are one of the most flavorful of all garden greens, plus they're easy to grow and can take the heat and the cold better than most.

Years ago my wife and I planted mustard just to see how it grew. We planted a large-leafed type that made broad plants that reached almost to my knee. The raw leaves were spicy, with a horseradish flavor, but when boiled or sautéed they were mild and delicious, with excellent flavor and a very pleasant texture.

There are quite a few varieties of mustard you can grow, including some intended for salads, but I generally find the uncooked greens too biting to be enjoyable—unless I need to clear my sinuses.

My favorite types are the large-leafed plants that provide plenty of greens for our large family. Crinkly types seem to be weaker and more prone to aphid attacks. In the garden, mustard is quite easy to grow and thrives on minimal care. The seeds look like small radish or cabbage seeds. I plant them in rows a couple feet apart, sprinkling them every few inches, then covering them with no more than a half-inch of loose soil. Seedlings emerge in a few days, looking just like other members of the brassica family. When they're an inch or two tall and have their true leaves, thin them to a couple inches apart and eat the thinnings in salads or stir-fries. Thin progressively, so the plants are a foot or more apart in the rows at full-size. They grow big and thick without the extra competition.

Mustard grows on so-so soil but is happier on rich soil with some compost. It responds well to foliar feeding. If you make a nice, loose bed before planting and rake in some compost, that should keep it happy through the gardening season.

Mustard will coast through light frosts. In South Florida, plant mustard from October through January. In North Florida, plant it in early November for a fall crop, then again in February for a spring crop.

Nematodes usually don't like mustard, so it's a good crop to plant in between crops that suffer from nematode infestations, such as okra and tomatoes. It's also a good cover crop in general, making a decent amount of biomass you can plow under if you don't get around to eating it all.

If you want to make your own condiment mustard, just let the plants go to seed. After a few months in the garden, mustard sends up tall stalks covered in little bright-yellow blooms. After blooming, thin little seed pods soon emerge, then dry on the stalk some weeks later. When they do, it's time to harvest. I take a big bowl to the garden and crumble the seed pods over it. Don't wait too long, because the pods shatter and spread seeds all over your garden if you don't get to them on time. We usually harvest seeds in a few successive harvests. The bowl ends up filling with lots of little seeds and pieces of papery pod. Mustard seeds are easy to winnow. Just let them drop from one container into another in front of a small fan set on "low", or you roll the seeds around and use your breath to blow out the little pod pieces.

I admit to not having made my own mustard yet, or I'd give you a recipe. We usually save seeds and re-plant, but our last round of mustard—which we were going to let go to seed and make condiment mustard from so I could write about it—was a new crinkly type we were testing. It succumbed to aphids and the heat before giving us seeds, so you're on your own making mustard.

Mustard is a forgiving green with good nutritional qualities. It's simple to direct-seed in the garden and takes a wide range of soils and temperatures. It's also resistant to pests and may even repel some of them. Florida Broadleaf is the type I recommend for now.

Pak Choi

Pak Choi is a cool-season green from China. Plant and grow it like you would its relative mustard. Unlike mustard, it has thick, crunchy stems that are great in stir-fries. It also has a milder flavor than mustard and can be eaten raw without causing your sinuses to empty. I started transplants of pak choi in January and planted them out with great success in February. They are quite easy to grow and great for Asian cooking, though not all of my children like them. We have not been able to save seeds, as the plants die after a few months of production without blooming.

Sweet Potato Leaves

Do not overlook the value of sweet potato leaves as a green vegetable. See calorie crop section above for notes on growing sweet potatoes.

Other Useful Crops

Bamboo (Clumping)

Though most bamboo shoots can be processed and eaten as a minor edible, bamboo also has many uses in the garden. Cane pole types of bamboo make excellent garden stakes and trellises as well as fishing poles. Smaller diameter bamboos can also be used to make decent smoking pipes in a pinch. Cut a piece of 1" or so cane an inch and a half above a joint, then drill an angled hole just above the joint down towards the bottom of the pipe bowl and insert a little piece of hollow bamboo for a pipe stem. You can make one in a few minutes with power tools or in a little less than an hour without.

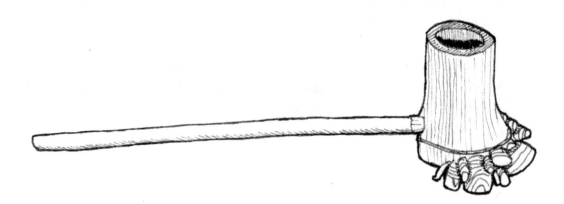

Mark Twain would be proud of this homemade bamboo pipe.
(Drawing by my eldest son)

Larger bamboo varieties are great for all manner of building projects, though they take up a lot more space in your yard. Stick to clumping bamboos as the running types will take over. I accidentally planted running bamboo on a previous homestead, which turned into a nightmare. When I mentioned this on a livestream, someone asked me how I eventually got them under control. My answer? I sold the property!

Basil

Basil is easy to grow from seed. It likes a little cooler weather and some shade and cannot take frost. They self-seed regularly and grow well in pots. Pinch off the bloom spikes to keep leaf production going or just let some of them go to seed and die, then save the seeds for next year's basil. Basil does not like freezing weather, so only plant it after all danger of frost. You can easily keep some basil growing year-round in South Florida. Richer soil is better—they love being in pots.

Chayote

Chayote are a bizarre perennial squash that tastes like a cross between cucumbers and a mild pear. It is sometimes called the "vegetable pear". I like growing them, but my family is not particularly fond of them. It is edible raw or cooked and is a tropical vegetable so it cannot take frosts. You can find chayote for sale in many supermarkets. Buy one or ten, take them home, then put them on your counter or someplace warm to sprout.

The entire fruit is the seed, so do not cut it open. Just let it sit until a vine starts emerging from the crevice at one end. Then, provided the danger of frost has passed, you can plant it out in your yard or garden by something it can climb. Bury them on their sides about 2/3" deep in the soil, and the

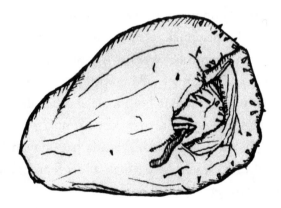

Sprouting chayote squash look like a monstrous birth in progress.
(Drawing by my eldest son)

vine will grow out and start climbing. About half the ones I plant in Florida just rot in the ground, but the ones that catch grow vigorously.

Chayote do not set fruit until late summer or fall, and then they'll make an abundance of chayote squash, often high up into the trees if they can get there. Freezes will take the vines to the ground, but they often grow back again. I mulched mine and they would re-sprout as soon as things warmed up again in spring, then travel back up the pomegranate tree I had supporting them. Save some fruit before your first frost if you are in the northern part of the state so you can plant more in the spring.

Cucumbers

Cucumbers are mostly water, but they are good for morale. The garden cukes we are familiar with require good soil, regular water, a trellis, and good care to produce well. They don't really like Florida all that much, unfortunately. I find the pickling types do better than the large Straight 8 types and I prefer their flavor and thinner skin. Plant 3–5 cucumber seeds in little hills by a trellis in spring after all danger of frost. Give them about 4' between hills. Transplanted cucumbers usually do not do as well as direct-seeded ones. Bury some compost or something nitrogenous in the hills before you plant them and they'll be happier. Cucumbers also thrive on places where there's been a fire—they enjoy a bit of wood ashes. Regular watering is important, as well as staying on top of insect problems.

All that said, I usually do not bother with "normal" cucumbers in Florida. However, their invasive perennial relative, *Coccinea grandis* is super easy to grow and produces continuously for years. It's also known as the "ivy gourd" or sometimes "tindoora" if you are talking with Indians. They can be found occasionally in the wild and come both male and female. Only the latter fruits and it does not require a mate to make cucumbers. The resultant seeds will be sterile as well, which is good. Florida has enough invasive plants creeping around already. If you have a male and a female, the seeds will be viable and are likely to get spread all over the place.

Female plants are propagated easily via cuttings, which root readily in moist soil in a shady spot. The plants have little or no pest issues and produce in dry or wet conditions, producing large white blooms that give way to small mottled green cucumbers. If the cucumbers sit on the vine too long, they turn into an inedible sour, red mush. This vegetable is usually cooked, but I

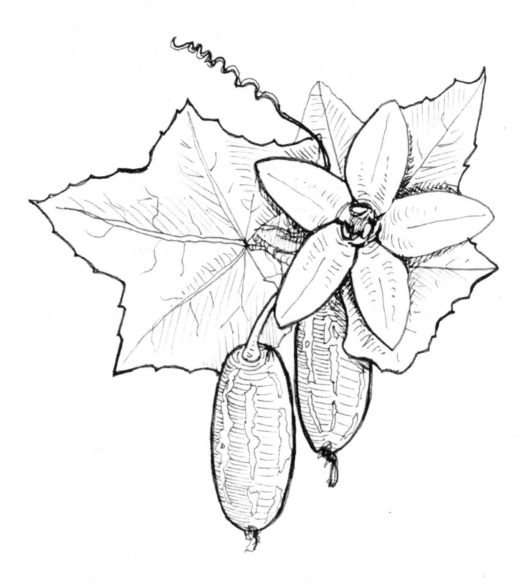

The delicate beauty of ivy gourd hides its terrifyingly invasive nature.

also like them raw or pickled. You can watch my wife pickle them in one of our YouTube videos. The best sources for planting material are Indians (from India) or plant geeks. You may have to show the former a picture of the plant in order to explain what you are looking for, as the Indian names seem to vary. I got my first one from the fence of a gas station in Anthony, Florida, though I ate them as a child thanks to the Indian family living across the street from my family when we were growing up. Interestingly, I visited the neighbor to their house a couple of years ago and found there were STILL ivy gourd cucumbers growing on the fence even though the Indian family had moved out almost two decades before. This means it is a bad, bad, bad invasive. So don't plant it.

Note: if you want to grow this awful and super productive thing, do not buy *Coccinea grandis* seeds on eBay. Multiple people have tried and then written me to say the seeds failed to germinate. This may be because they are harvested from female plants or just because there are a ton of scammers on eBay. Or maybe the state of Florida is selling bum seeds to lawbreakers and using the proceeds to buy more RoundUp.

Finally, a female ivy gourd in your garden, if kept from wandering off, can be controlled and generally won't be too invasive, but woe unto the gardener who lets it run out of control! You will fight it forever! Every joint of the plant can root in the ground and doesn't care about drought, bad soil, or property lines. And of course, I don't recommend it at all, because the State of Florida would not appreciate me doing so.

Eggplant

Eggplants can do well in Florida. Another neighbor of mine as a kid, "Aunt" Linda Randazzo, had a beautiful eggplant growing in her yard when I used to play with her son Ray. It was the first time I ever saw an eggplant, and I had no idea what it was or what they tasted like, but I was amazed by the beauty of the plant and its fruit. Eggplant can be grown easily from seeds or transplants and likes warm weather, good soil, and a decent amount of water. They also seem to like mulch. They take a while to get moving, but will start making you eggplants within a couple of months. In North Florida, I would plant them in February and cover them if there's a frost, then plant them again in late October and hope to get a harvest before winter killed them. In South Florida, I would grow them year-round. They can take a little shade but not a lot, and regular feeding keeps them happy. The bushes can grow pretty large and make plenty of eggplant if they are happy, but if they are not, they sit and stay shrimpy and give up on you. This isn't the easiest plant to grow, but it isn't the hardest either. It's not a great survival crop, but my wife and I love them sautéed in coconut oil with some salt and garlic powder, so we grow them when we have space.

Everglades Tomato

The Everglades tomato is the only tomato in Florida that grows happily without bringing gardeners pain, suffering, and loss. It is sweet and abundant, though tiny, and self-seeds happily and grows again. Plant after danger of frost in North Florida and just about year-round in South Florida.

The dead heat of summer may keep it from producing a lot, but as the weather cools they will produce more fruit for you. Frosts will kill them, but you'll often get them again from fallen tomatoes, sometimes in the most interesting places.

Ginger and Turmeric

All you need to grow ginger and turmeric are some fresh roots with living "eyes" on them. The eyes are growth buds from which the green shoots grow. Chances are you won't even have to buy roots or starts from a seed company, as many grocery stores—particularly organic markets—stock fresh roots right in the produce section. Just watch to make sure the eyes aren't cut off, as I've seen done on some imported Chinese ginger roots.

If you're interested in growing ginger to sell, you'll likely be better off buying clean seed roots from someone, though I've never had trouble with any of the plants I've started from grocery store or farmer's market roots.

Ginger roots are quite a bit larger than turmeric roots so I break them up into a few pieces that each have at least 3 or 4 eyes on them. Turmeric roots I usually plant entire unless they're in a clump, then I break them up. Don't let the roots sit around on your counter and dry out for too long or they won't grow. Just take them and plant them right into the soil if you live in a warm area or into a big pot if you don't. Then wait—it sometimes takes a long time for ginger to send up shoots. Plant fall through spring. I plant mine at about 3–4" depth in loosened soil.

Ginger and turmeric are perennials with a growing season and a dormant season. In spring shoots emerge from the ground when the weather is nice and warm. Ginger pops up faster. Turmeric is a slowpoke. The plants wait until a couple of warm months pass then really get started in summer. If you plant roots and they don't come up right away, don't worry—as I said, they have a dormancy period. When their internal timers say "sprout!", they'll sprout.

Ginger and turmeric do not like high temperatures or harsh sunlight. They sunburned badly in my North Florida garden if I didn't plant them in the shade. Instead, I grew them beneath the fruit trees in my food forest where they produced quite happily, though I didn't really follow the rules on feeding and watering. They can take a lot of neglect and not die, but they'll produce much better—and faster—if you feed and water them regularly.

Ginger and turmeric burn if you give them too much fertilizer and grow more leaves than roots if they get too much nitrogen. My advice is to plant them in good soil and load the plants up with compost. Mulching is great.

Commercial growers hill up ginger (much as you would potatoes) a few times over the growing season to ensure well-shaped roots and plenty of growth; however, I haven't done this and it hasn't been necessary. Maybe one day I'll do so as an experiment and see if the yields improve.

Ginger and turmeric like regular watering but do not like to sit in water or constantly wet soil. When the weather is cool (say, below around 70°F), the plants just sit around without doing much. When it gets hot outside (say, over 90°F), they also slow down. I had both conditions in North Florida, but keeping them in the shade moderated things quite a bit and kept them going.

Ginger and turmeric never had any real pest or disease problems in my Florida gardens. A few leaves may get gnawed now and again, but the plants usually take care of themselves.

In November ginger and turmeric leaves yellow and die back to the ground whether it freezes or not. If it freezes, all the aboveground growth is knocked down faster, but even if it doesn't they will go dormant. This is the time to harvest roots. A lot of the root development takes place in the last little bit before the plants die down so don't be too eager to harvest. I allowed my plants to form clumps and didn't harvest until the second year.

When I did harvest, I got plenty of roots from each clump and would just leave a few pieces in the hole after harvesting so they'd come back again in the spring. Ginger is more productive for me than turmeric, with much larger roots. Sometimes I would just dig out a chunk of ginger root from one of my clumps—any time in the year—when we needed some for a recipe or an upset stomach. Turmeric I usually harvested in one fell swoop after letting it grow for a couple of years into a respectable clump.

When you harvest, try to be gentle with the roots. Earlier in the season they are more delicate due to the new growth. This is sometimes called "baby ginger". If you pull them later after the tops die in the fall/winter, ginger and turmeric have tougher roots.

If you want to skip all that work of growing in the ground, just grow ginger or turmeric in a large pot. It's quite forgiving. Just don't overwater or let it dry all the way out.

Give ginger and turmeric a try, and you'll be growing them for life. As a bonus, you can use the leaves for tea or added to soup like bay leaves for a little tropical zip.

Hot Peppers

Hot peppers are a wonderful addition to the table. They are both good for flavoring and good for your health. We love jalapeños and cayenne peppers, both added to dishes and made into salsas and hot sauces. Dried, cayenne peppers can be powdered in a cheap espresso grinder to make "red pepper". Or you can crush dried cayenne peppers for crushed red pepper, which is marvelous on pizza. I also did this with habaneros, but it made the pizzas almost too spicy to eat. I don't recommend hanging up peppers to dry in Florida as our state is humid enough to spoil peppers, but slitting and drying them on a mat in the sun or in a dehydrator works well.

Hot peppers are a tropical crop and cannot take frost. In South Florida, hot peppers can grow into shrubs that live and produce for multiple years. I had a habanero do that for me and it produced more peppers than we could use without destroying our tastebuds and digestive tracts forever. Paprika/Pimento peppers are also easy to grow and add great spice to your food without the heat. I do not grow the common Hungarian Wax pepper because I do not like the flavor, so you're on your own with that one.

In Central and North Florida, your pepper plants may be killed by frost, though mulched pepper plants sometimes grow back from the roots. Potted hot peppers can be put in a sheltered location on icy nights and survive for multiple years. Bell peppers are touchy and hard to grow in Florida so we don't bother with them.

Okra

Okra is a heavy producer, though the slimy pods are an acquired taste. They can be eaten raw or cooked. Rachel likes to fry them until they get a little crispy, then serve them, though the kids and I often eat the sweet pods right in the garden. Okra cannot take frost, but it can take the heat. The plants can be planted after frost and right through the summer in North and Central

Florida and year-round in South Florida. Don't plant them on the same ground twice in a row as they are very susceptible to nematodes destroying their roots. Aphids can be a problem as well, though the ladybugs are often close behind. Keep okra picked almost daily or the pods will get too hard and woody to eat. If you let some pods dry on the plants, you'll get plenty of seeds for the next planting. Just pick one bush to leave alone, as letting the pods go to seed will bring your regular harvest of green pods to an end.

Papaya

Papaya are very easy to grow from seed. Just take the guts out of a store-bought papaya and plant some of the slop in a spot you want a papaya tree. Plant them in stations 6' apart. When the seedlings come up in 2–4 weeks, let them grow to a few inches tall then thin all but the strongest on the hill. Alternatively, you can leave three papayas on each station. Here's why: papayas are a little complicated, as they come in male, female, and hermaphroditic plants. The latter two will produce fruit, but the males only produce blooms. Having a male or two around for pollination is a good idea,

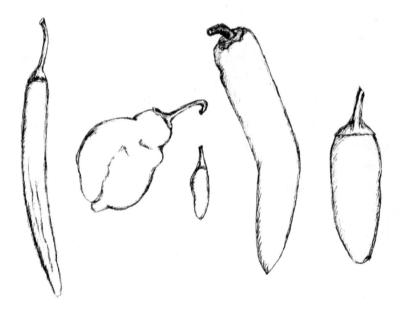

Cayenne, Caribbean seasoning pepper, tabasco, Hungarian wax, and jalapeño.
(Drawing by my 14-year-old daughter)

but you want more of your trees to be females or hermaphrodites—hence leaving three trees to grow in each station. Once they bloom, it is easy to tell if papayas are male or female and you can cut down the two trees you don't want.

Papayas are a tropical tree and can grow throughout the state with some work. In the northern half away from the shore, they tend to get knocked to the ground by frosts and do not recover well, but if you can keep them protected or have a lucky winter, you'll get good fruit, especially because the loathsome papaya fruit wasp does not live up there. In south Florida you can grow papayas year round and keep planting more, but the wasp will often ruin the fruit. The female wasp stings green fruit and lays her eggs inside. When the fruits ripen and you cut them open, they are rotten inside and filled with grubs. Bagging them early will keep her out, but it is a lot of work. I would rather just plant a lot of trees here and there and burn any infected fruit I find.

If well-fed and watered, papaya trees can produce within a year. They are greedy plants and want lots of water and food to grow well. You almost cannot overfeed them, but if their roots stay soaked for more than a day or so they often rot and die, so keep them well-watered, but also well-drained.

Green papayas are edible cooked or raw in Thai salad. Some people are allergic to the sap of green papayas, so be careful not to eat too much unless you know you can take it. A pregnant woman should avoid papayas altogether as some enzymes in them can cause her to abort her unborn child. Green papayas are a good cooked vegetable when peeled and the insides removed. Chop and sauté or cook in stews. A good ripe papaya is like a tree melon, delicious served with breakfast.

Sugarcane

Sugarcane is easy to grow in Florida and does not require flooded conditions to produce. I cover it in the appendix of *Totally Crazy Easy Florida Gardening*, but in short, all you need is a good hunk of sugarcane with a few intact nodes (those are the joints in the cane). Since sugarcane is usually harvested in the fall, that's the time you're likely to see the canes for sale. Most grocery stores don't carry sugarcane, but a lot of farm stands do in the fall—and fall is when you want to plant, at least in North Florida. Buy a couple of stout canes (they're usually 5–6 feet long with about 8–12 nodes, depending on the cultivar), and you're well on your way. When you get home, cut your canes into segments with at least 3–4 nodes each, pick a good spot to plant them, then put those pieces on their sides about 4–6 inches down, and cover them up well.

All winter, those pieces will sit down there in the ground until the soil warms up in the spring. When I planted sugarcane in a North Florida November, the plants would pop up for me sometime in March or April. For each cane you bury, you'll usually get a couple of good shoots emerging from the ground. If you really don't want to trust the earth to take care of your little baby sugarcane plants, you can just stick some chunks of cane in pots with a node or two beneath the dirt and keep them someplace that doesn't freeze, like a sunroom. They'll grow. When my baby sugarcane plants appeared in the spring and I was sure it wasn't going to freeze again I would fertilize them with chicken manure. You can also use lawn fertilizer. (They're a grass—they like lots of nitrogen.) Throughout the summer they'll get nice and tall, and sometime in July or August you'll really see the canes starting to thicken up, but don't chop them yet (unless you really can't stand to wait).

In North Florida, wait until it's just about time for the first frost of fall or winter, then go cut the canes down so you'll get the largest harvest possible. If you don't cut them down and you get a freeze, you're going to lose all the above ground growth and you may even lose the plants. Harvest by cutting the canes down close to the ground, and then put the sugarcane roots to bed for the winter by mulching over them with some rough material. Leaves are good for this, but probably any mulch would work fine. My sugarcane came back even when I barely mulched over the roots. In its second year, sugarcane will bunch out and usually give you a few more canes than it did the first year.

In South Florida, just bury some canes whenever you have them and keep them fed and watered. Unless you have a sugarcane press, you'll have to enjoy your cane by peeling pieces of the cane and chewing the sugar out of it. They're delicious. Don't try using your home juicer on it. I had a great one and it couldn't handle the hard fibers inside. A cheap juicer will burst into flames, melt, shoot sparks, implode, then violently explode if you try to run sugarcane through it. We have chopped up cane and boiled it to get the sugar out, then boiled the juice down into cane syrup. It's labor-intensive and probably not nearly as efficient as having cane juice, though. A month ago I fermented some cane juice to see if I could make a drinkable beer. Two weeks later, I drank it. It was… drinkable.

Tobacco

I cover tobacco growing and curing in depth in my booklet *The Survival Gardener's Guide to Growing Tobacco*, but I'll give you the short version here. It's easy to grow but takes a little work to get started and a lot of work to get good leaves. I sometimes smoke homegrown tobacco dried green on the dash of my car, but I'm hardcore. It does not taste good that way.

Tobacco is a little tricky to start because the seeds are very tiny and require light and moisture to germinate. What this means in practice is that you have to sprinkle the seeds on top of the soil and keep them well lit and moist at the same time. Since the seeds are so tiny, they dry out quickly in the sun and new shoots will wither away and disappear on a hot day if you aren't watching out for them. My preferred planting method is to simply fill one of my wood planting flats with fine potting soil. You can also use plastic trays or whatever holds soil—just make sure it drains well. Even egg cartons with added nail holes for drainage will work.

Once I have my planting flat, I place it in indirect sunlight (my back porch is perfect) and then sprinkle tobacco seeds generously across the surface of the soil. I then mist it well with a spray bottle of water. Then, every day, multiple times a day, I mist the surface again as I think about it. This goes on for usually 10–14 days until I see lots of little shoots popping up and then I keep misting those. Tobacco sprouts are really, really tiny—a gardener almost needs to get out his magnifying glass to see them when they first emerge from the soil.

Another method for germinating tobacco seeds is to simply mist the flat and then cover it with plastic wrap to keep in the moisture and cut down on your need to water. I do recommend taking it off now and again to avoid mold issues. Also be careful not to leave a plastic-wrapped flat in the sun. That'll roast your baby tobacco plants. Within a week or two, the little plants will get bigger. In a month or so, they'll likely be an inch or so in height. Give each little plant more space and their growth rate will be much higher. Once your baby tobacco plants are up and growing, thin them out with a pair of hair scissors to give each little plant about an inch of space. As they get to around 1" tall, thin again or transplant them to another new flat at 4" spacing. A spoon makes a good trowel for tiny tobacco plants. As the plants grow, I try to make sure they get more direct sunlight during the day so they can adapt before making their way into my garden.

Let your starts reach 2–4" before planting them out in the tobacco patch. Tobacco transplants easily, though it'll usually look sad for the first few days after transplanting. This is because the leaves are large and soft and will lose their moisture because of root disturbance. Keep them well watered and they'll recover. I've discovered that tobacco transplants often live even without a good bit of their root mass unless it's really hot outside—they're tough plants. When you transplant the tobacco, put it in the ground with at least 2' spacing between plants. Some varieties of tobacco have very large leaves—if you're growing those, give them even more space. It's not a good idea to pack them too close and have them running over each other. If you want to give your tobacco a little extra help at the onset, water them with some foliar fertilizer when they're planted out. Good soil also grows better plants.

Tobacco is a warm-season crop that cannot take the cold. Plant it out in spring after all danger of frost has passed and you'll be in a good shape.

Whatever you do, as long as they get some nutrition, your plants will get big (about 5'). At this point, you can start picking nice leaves, though I usually sneak some early on to dry and smoke.

The biggest tobacco pest I've faced is the hornworm. Pick them off and kill them as soon as you see them as they will strip your plants bare. Another pest I've dealt with is an ugly green, yellow or light brown caterpillar called the tobacco budworm. It feeds almost exclusively on the buds and seed pods of tobacco plants and will take out next year's seed supply in a hurry.

If leaves get chewed up, they go in my "pipe and cigarette" tobacco pile, if they're broad and intact, they go in my "attempt to make cigars again" pile.

If you top your plants when they start to set flowers (just go ahead and chop off the top foot or two of the plant), the bottom leaves will fill out and ripen up better than if you let the flowers grow and set seed pods.

When the bottom leaves start to yellow and/or brown on my tobacco plants, I go down the row and snap them off at the base with a little twist, gathering them into a bundle as I go. Some growers will also harvest the entire plant at once, chopping it at the base. I prefer to pick the good leaves off for my cigars and pipes and leave the rest for the compost heap or for later processing for friends who smoke cigarettes. Once I have a good little stack of tobacco leaves, I thread a big needle with some strong thread and pierce the stems at the bases of the leaves, then string them up in the rafters of my barn to dry. I've also seen tobacco tied in bundles on sticks, pierced and hung or just spread out to dry (in Turkey they spread the leaves on roofs).

Methods for curing tobacco abound, yet I've found just stringing the leaves on thread and hanging them in my barn for a year makes them taste pretty good. For barter purposes, just dry the tobacco nicely, then pack it away for later use. The main thing that makes tobacco taste better is a good drying process, followed by a time of aging. The tobacco you dried and hung up last year will taste better than the tobacco you're drying right now. Two-year old tobacco is even better. Dried leaves can later be crumbled for cigarettes or pipe tobacco or made into chewing tobacco. If you've managed to keep your leaves intact, they can also be rolled into cigars.

In South Florida you can grow tobacco year round, but in North Florida you are limited to frost-free months.

Now that we've moved on through the garden crops, let's take a look at a few wild edibles you can forage in the Sunshine State.

Wild Amaranth

American persimmon blooms, leaves, and fruit

Chapter 4

WILD FLORIDA EDIBLES

Florida has an abundance of wild edibles that can stand in for regular crops. Many have stronger flavors or are tougher, but they make up for it with high nutrition levels for no work.

Here are a few that may be growing in your neighborhood.

Amaranth

Various wild amaranths grow in disturbed areas across Florida, particularly in pastures and gardens. Spiny pigweed is the worst of them but is still edible. Once you can identify one type of amaranth, you'll see them everywhere.

Cook the leaves before eating, as they are high in oxalic acid. They are great stir-fried with eggs and in fried rice.

American Persimmon

American persimmon trees are common in hardwood forests and sometimes in scrubland in the Northern half of the state. Trees may be male or female. The male trees do not make fruit but are necessary for pollinating the female trees. I have saved many persimmons while doing property analyses for clients, as they are not well known and often get cleared when people are improving land. When I point them out, people are glad to know they had fruit they hadn't seen before.

Once you can spot them, you'll see them regularly. The fruit are small and very awful and astringent until fully ripe and squishy soft, then they are delightful. As my son said to me, "If you ever taste an unripe persimmon, you're like: cut that tree down NOW!" As with many wild foods, knowing when it is ready makes all the difference.

Blackberries

Various blackberries and their relatives grow wild in Central and North Florida. There are no poisonous lookalikes.

Blueberries

Though Florida is not known for its wild blueberries, there are multiple different species—and edible relatives, such as sparkleberry and deerberry—in the wild. Some make tiny little plants that produce tiny berries bursting with flavor. Others are taller and make fruit ranging from sweet to tart. Wild blueberries are common in the Northern half of the state and can usually be found in association with pine trees on poor, sandy, acid soils.

Identification of plants is easy in spring when they make their easy-to-recognize bell-shaped blooms, and later in the year when they set bluish-black or purple fruit.

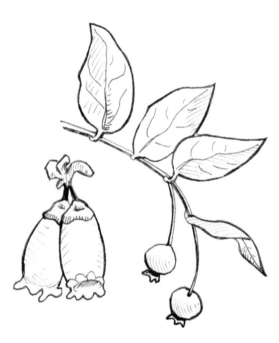

Blackberries   *Blueberry leaves, blooms, and fruit*

Cocoplums

Along the warm coast of Southern Florida you will often find cocoplums for the picking. They come in black and white variants, with the latter usually showing a blush of pink. The plants are handsome and often used as hedges in my home town of Ft. Lauderdale.

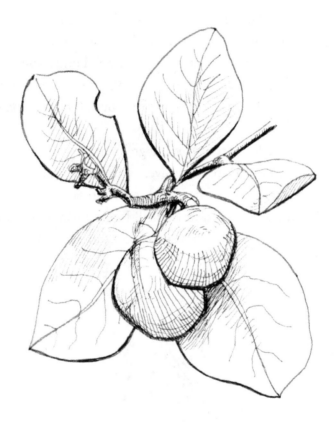

Cocoplums

The fruit ranges from thin-fleshed and somewhat astringent to large and sweet. When you find a good one, take some seeds home and plant them. Germination takes 2–3 months, but they mostly come up.

Beautyberry

Have you ever seen those strange wild shrubs with tiny berries that look as pink-purple as the Barbie aisle at Toys 'R' Us? The stems are square, and the berries cluster around them in repeating bunches. Most of the people I talk to think they're poisonous, but the American Beautyberry isn't even remotely dangerous. The berries, though rather bland and mealy, are relished by my children and rumored to make good jelly. Even if you don't eat them, they're great food for chickens and other birds. I pick them when hiking. Some plants have berries that taste better than others, so if you get some so-so ones, don't give up.

Bitter Gourd

A small, wild form of bitter gourd grows all over Florida and produces weird orange fruits. Sometimes called Balsam Pear, you'll hear stories about how they are poisonous, but most of the plant won't bother you. Green fruits can be chopped and sautéed as well as young greens. The red pulp can be sucked off the seeds inside ripe orange fruit, but do not eat the fruit or the seeds inside as they can cause stomach upset.

Young greens are less bitter than the green fruits and can disappear into cooked greens without being offensive. The green fruits are an acquired taste. I read that they can be sliced and soaked in salt brine before cooking to reduce bitterness, so I tried it, but still found them almost too bitter to eat. Reportedly good for diabetics and cancer sufferers.

Bitter Gourd

Shepherd's Needle

Also known as Bidens alba, shepherd's needles are one of the most irritating weeds in Florida yards—yet without them, our native bees and butterflies would suffer. The flowers look little daisies… which mature into little prickly clusters of black needle-like seeds with barbed hooks on them.

Shepherd's Needle

These seeds love socks like hornworms love tomatoes. Here's the up side of these persistent garden pests: their greens are nutritious and delicious when stir-fried. I regularly add them to my scrambled eggs. Very good.

Simpson Stoppers

The Simpson Stopper is a native shrub often used as a hedge plant. In summer it bears a crop of oval red berries that can get almost an inch long. When fully ripe, the berries are pleasantly sweet with a bitter grapefruit aftertaste that's rather nice.

Some people don't like the bitterness, but I find it similar to Campari. I love Campari. If you haven't tried Campari, buy a bottle. Drink it on ice (though not all at once... that way lies headaches). Then, if you like that, go eat some Simpson Stoppers. I planted multiple bushes in my yard, probably while under the influence.

Smilax

Also known as "greenbriers", or "briars", or "THOSE BLANKETY-BLANK THORNY THINGS", smilax is a relative of asparagus with delicious shoots. Use like asparagus. Excellent sautéed in garlic and butter. Make sure you don't have a bitter type before committing to it—taste a little raw to make sure! There are a variety of species growing in Florida.

People hate how thorny they are, but I love to visit the woods in spring when the shoots emerge from the ground and gather bundles for the table.

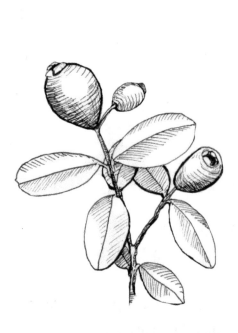

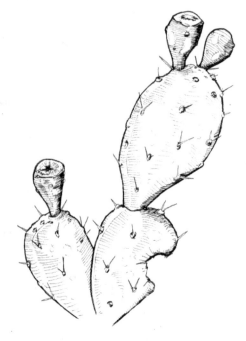

Simpson Stoppers   *Prickly Pear*

Snap them off where they break easily on the stem, usually 6" to a foot below the growing tip. The hard roots can be dug and boiled for starch but are very fibrous and hard to eat.

Thistle

Thistle leaves are nutritious but bitter. Cut off the spiny parts of the leaves and the center stem and sauté or add to stews.

Wild Grapes

In the northern half of Florida, there are a few different species of wild grapes, of which wild muscadines are the most common. The leaves are edible cooked but aren't anything to write home about; however, the fruit can be quite good.

Some wild grapes are sweet, others are quite tart and acidic. All make great jam when you add some sugar, remove the seeds and cook them down. Watch for grapes in summer and fall. Many vines won't have any at all, as they are male and do not produce fruit, but when you find one covered in fruit, remember where it is because it is a female and will produce for years. Add wild grape leaves to homemade pickles to keep cukes crisp.

Prickly Pear

There are various pad cactus (*Opuntia spp.*) growing in Florida, known colloquially as "prickly pears". All are edible, though some are better than others.

Pick young and somewhat tender pads and roast them over a fire to burn off the spines, then slice them up and cook them. Pad cactus also have edible fruit. Just watch out for the spines, especially the tiny glochid spines that will sting and itch for days if you pick up a cactus with your bare hands.

Purslane

Everyone knows purslane's edibility. You'll find it in broken ground and sunny areas, often by roadsides and paths. The leaves can make your throat a little scratchy raw so I cook them first. High in Omega-3 fatty acids.

Wild Yams

Dioscorea alata, a.k.a. the greater yam or winged yam, is loose in the Florida woods and can sometimes be found on roadsides and in vacant lots. Keep an eye out for it and do not confuse it with the poisonous air potato (*D. bulbifera*). Here is a drawing I did to show the difference between the leaves and the bulbils of the two species:

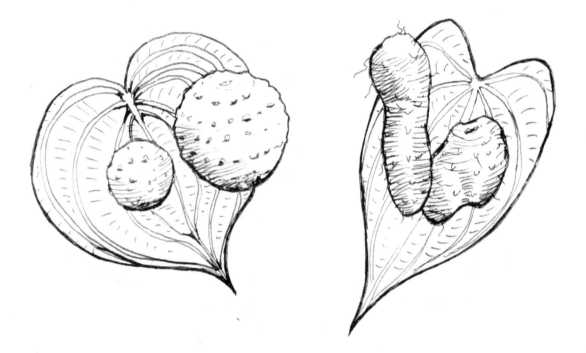

D. bulbifera *bulbils and leaf on left,* D. alata *bulbils and leaf on right.*

Note the rounder bulbils on the *D. bulbifera* and the heart-shaped leaves. *D. alata* leaves are more arrowhead-like and the dangling bulbils are darker and misshapen, never nice and round. If you find *D. alata* in the wild, you could take the bulbils home and plant them, or dig and divide the roots for the same purpose. They are the best wild edible in the state for caloric density.

This is just a brief overview of our wild edibles. There are many, many more. Green Deane's site www.eattheweeds.com is the best online resource for learning about Florida's wild edible plants. One day I may write a book on the topic, as many have asked me to do, but this short chapter will have to suffice for now.

Now that we've covered staple crops, nutrition crops and some of our wild edibles, let's take a look at watering and feeding your gardens.

Chapter 5

FEEDING AND WATERING MADE SIMPLE

Let's face it: Florida's "soil" is the main thing Yankees complain about when they move down here and attempt to grow their touchy Yankee crops on our beautiful piece of paradise.

The soil is indeed a problem. It isn't even soil. Though there are a few places in Florida with muck soils or nice sandy loams or even clay, most of the state is a big sandbox. It's hot, dry, fast-draining stuff that eats organic matter overnight. People often ask me how to improve their soils. It's tough! You're fighting against geology. Organic matter burns out of sandy soils and fertilizers leach through and run off faster than you can say "eutrophication". Add to that our hot and humid climate that provides perfect conditions for decomposition and you are fighting an uphill battle. If you're growing long-term perennials, deep mulching can build a nice bit of organic matter quickly and keep it there, so long as you keep mulching year after year, but if you leave that area alone for a while or till it up, in a year or so you'd never know it had been improved. There's a spot in my parents' backyard where I dumped compost and bagged soil and peat moss for years. It looks like the Sahara now. Geology wins. This doesn't mean it's hopeless, it just means you need to work with what you have. Sand has some great benefits. It drains well, it's very easy to weed and dig and you can mix your own concrete without purchasing sand. Sweet potatoes, carrots and yams don't mind it a bit and will make nice, well-shaped roots that are easy to dig. Sand is also good when you want to kill fire ants. Just pour a pot of boiling water right into the middle of a nest and it will stream and steam right down through and kill the queen and all her little maggoty babies in seconds.

I love sand. There, I said it. I confess it. I love it. It's so FAST to dig. I have made gardens in hard red rocky clay and it was backbreaking work. Not in Florida! You can tear up your backyard and plant it in a weekend if you're a good digger.

Yet it's not "soil" as we would like it to be. So what do we do about the sand? There are a few options.

Add Clay to Your Compost Pile

If you have a source of clay, add it to your compost regularly and it will help the humus "stick" for a much longer time. Compost made without clay disappears rapidly, but if you can add some clay, it will really help it last. Baseball diamond clay can sometimes be purchased from landscape suppliers and it's a good addition. You can also dig up veins of clay in parts of Florida and make it into a slurry and soak your compost with it. Alternatively, unscented cat litter is usually pure bentonite clay so you can buy a bag and sprinkle it in layers as you compost. I do not recommend adding used cat litter due to the risk of toxoplasmosis, which will turn you into a crazy cat lady.

I have not experimented with adding clay directly to my garden beds, but I intend to if I ever make it home to the Sunshine State.

Experiment with Biochar

Biochar, which is just a fancy word for charcoal, has shown much promise as a long-term stand in for humus in sandy soils. Burn your brush and extinguish it when it is still red embers, then soak the resultant coals in some fertilizer solution (urine, compost tea, chicken manure water, etc.) to "charge" it, then add that to your beds and see if it helps your plants grow. Pure, un-soaked char can suck up nutrients for a long time and cause your plants to starve so I don't recommend it. Some people smash charcoal into dust and add it to beds as well, which may work even better than bigger chunks. Instead of charging biochar, you can also just add fresh char to your compost piles so you end up with it in your gardens over time.

Keep Mulching

Like I said above, mulching will build up a decent humusy soil, but it takes a lot of mulch to cover a large garden so I usually don't do it except on select beds and around my fruit trees and perennial crops. The heat and rain of Florida break down mulch very quickly and you have to keep applying a lot of material to suppress weed growth and keep the soil going. If you have a smaller garden, it might be a good idea to try mulching some of your beds and leaving others un-mulched to see how they do side by side. I've had good luck sometimes and other times I've had pest issues due to the large amount of insects, snails and slugs that move into mulched garden beds.

One great benefit of mulch is that it keeps the soil cool and moist on hot days. It's just the amount of mulch required for large gardens that makes it tough to deal with. Getting your plants to grow quickly so they shade the soil provides a similar benefit, keeping plant roots from getting baked in the mid-day heat.

Foliar Feeding

I was talking with my friend Steve Solomon (author of *Gardening When it Counts*) about Florida sand one day and he said we sand gardeners might just want to consider the sand as more of a substrate for roots, rather like the gravel or rock wool in a hydroponics garden, and keep our crops fed via regular foliar feeding. I have done this and it works well. Products that have a good range of macro and micronutrients, such as MiracleGro or Dyna-Gro or various other weird soluble colored crystal fertilizers, will feed Florida crops quite well. Fish and seaweed fertilizers are a good organic alternative, as is my personal favorite nutrient solution which I call "Dave's Fetid Swamp Water".

To make Dave's Fetid Swamp Water, take a drum or a few five-gallon buckets and stuff some weeds and grass in them, then top off with water and let it rot down into a tea. You can also add a few quarts of urine per five-gallon bucket, if that doesn't freak you out, as it provides nitrogen and other nutrients. A cup of Epsom salts, moringa leaves, a tiny bit of Borax, alfalfa, fish guts, mimosa leaves and many other ingredients can also be added to this tea and will help feed your plants. I do not recommend cow or other ruminant manures as most of them are contaminated with long-term herbicides (look up Aminopyralid) used to control weeds—they'll often kill your garden before it even gets a good start. Let the mess rot down for a few weeks, stirring when you think about it, then strain some out and dilute it at least half-and-half with water to use on your gardens. It smells awful, but plants like it.

Don't use it on maturing leaf crops like lettuce that will go immediately to the table, because this tea is full of anaerobic bacteria, some of which can harm you. Corn LOVES DFSW. I poured it undiluted at the base of my corn plants and they grew excellently. Bananas also thrive on it undiluted. Some garden vegetables may be a little touchier, so you may thin it as much as 4 parts water to one part DFSW until you know what they can handle.

Urine is a good source of nitrogen, diluted about 6 parts water to one part urine. I have written about the Florida garden I once saw, lush, green, and happy, fed only on the owner's diluted urine. This isn't for everyone, but it sure does green up plants. Just don't give a lot of it to root or fruit crops that may fail to produce if they get too much nitrogen.

With all these options, you can also just soak the root zone around plants and they'll take up what they need.

Other Amendments

Liquid fertilizers aside, you can also just come to grips with the fact that it is remarkably hard to turn your sand into soil and simply go ahead and feed new beds every time you plant a new crop in them. Ashes are good for potassium and calcium, bone meal and manures are good for phosphorus (though Florida soils usually don't need any) and blood meal, cottonseed meal, alfalfa pellets/alfalfa meal, and even dog food are good sources of nitrogen. Compost usually provides a good mix of everything. Greensand and azomite are also good, though I have not experimented with them. Kelp meal is great for micronutrients but can be expensive. Adding a half inch of compost to new garden beds, along with whatever other amendments you can find, is usually enough to get you a good crop before it burns out. If you have no other options, a couple cups of "balanced" fertilizer like 10-10-10 (in Florida, often 10-0-10 is fine) can be mixed into a bed before planting. Read the labels on the bag for application instructions. I am not a fan of chemical fertilizers long term, but when you need food, you need food.

Green Manures

Another option that helps feed crops is to plant cover crops in between your regular crops, then turn them under or chop them down and plant what you want to eat. Black-eyed peas and mung beans can be planted after your spring harvests and they'll coast through the summer heat, then you can turn them under before they finish ripening their seeds and plant the beds. The next crop will benefit greatly from the increased organic matter and nitrogen that had been added to the soil.

In winter when it's cool, I mix wheat, rye, mustard, chick peas, and lentils together and plant beds with them. Most of my cover crops come from the bulk bins at the local organic market. It's cheaper than buying seed from a seed supplier, and the germination rates are usually pretty good. Sometimes I just plant a cover crop and chop some of it down as mulch and plant new seeds or transplants right into it.

Composting On Top of Beds

In *Compost Everything*, I shared my method of composting right on top of garden beds in a rotation:

> *In my vegetable gardens I pick one of my 4' x 12' beds and designate it as the compost pile for a year. On that bed go all the spent vegetable plants from the other garden plots, along with the weeds, kitchen scraps, rotten pumpkins, etc. A lot of fertility is gained by that space over the 365 days*

that the pile lies there and rots. At the end of the year, I might shovel the uncomposted waste in the bed over to the bed next door and garden where the pile had been... or I might just smash it down a bit, mulch on top, then plant vegetable transplants right into the heap ... (and) another benefit to throwing your scraps right onto a garden bed: it's less work that putting all your scraps in a designated composting area, then later taking the final product and wheeling it over to your garden beds. When you drop organic matter into an unused bed, it's right where it needs to be. Furthermore, have you ever seen how nice and green the weeds get around the edges of a compost pile? That's because some of the fertility in the pile is running off into the ground around your stack of compost. When you compost directly in a gardening area, you let the good material go straight down into the soil where you'll later be growing vegetables for your table.

This method works quite well, though is hard to do on a large scale.

Let's just run through various mulches and amendments one at a time so you get a feel for what each does.

Garden Amendments and Their Uses

Alfalfa

Alfalfa is a good source of nitrogen as well as being a stimulant of plant growth. Alfalfa meal or pellets can be forked in when establishing beds. Alfalfa hay makes a fast-decomposing mulch to feed plants from above.

Ammonia

Ammonia is a fast source of nitrogen. A few tablespoons in a gallon of water is strong enough for feeding. Water struggling plants with it for a quick boost. It's like throwing gas on a fire, so it's not a good long-term feeding solution.

Animal Carcasses

Bury deeply and plant over the top, or add small animal carcasses to the middle of an active compost pile. I planted a canistel tree over the body of a beloved pet bunny and it is thriving. The illustration is by my son, R.G.

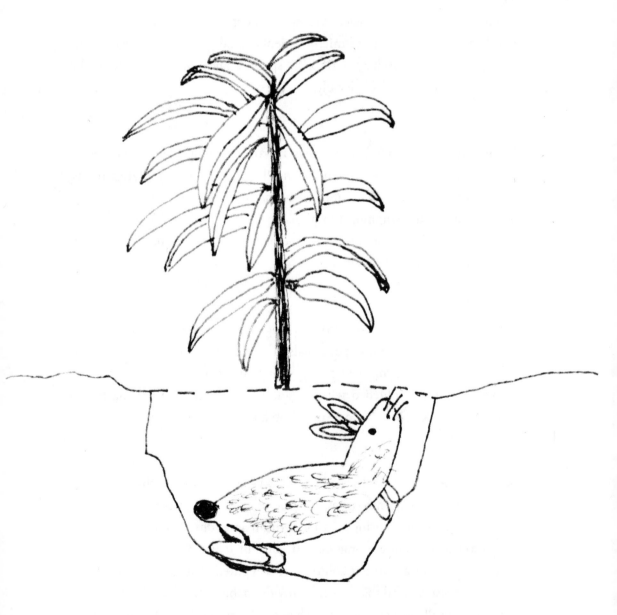

Our dear departed rabbit Caspian now resides beneath a young canistel seedling (Drawing by my 9-year-old son).

Ashes

Ashes are a good source of calcium and potassium, as well as various trace minerals. Do not add too much as it will raise the pH of your soil and cause nutritional issues in your plants if over-applied. Add more in acidic pineland soils and less in areas originally consisting of healthy, mixed-hardwood forests.

Azomite

Azomite® is mined from ancient volcanic ash deposits in Utah and provides a wide range of slow-release micronutrients. Many gardeners swear by it, adding as much as 100 lbs per 10' x 10' space. I have not tried it but would if we had a supply available locally.

Bat Guano

Apparently, you can buy bat guano as a fertilizer, though I've never seen it in Florida. I'm sure Corona-chan has not helped sales either. Bat guano is an excellent course of nitrogen, phosphorus and potassium, as well as trace nutrients including sulphur. On a related note, I read on Wikipedia that "the nest of the Peruvian booby is made of almost pure guano." Wow, just wow. Nice parenting, booby.

Banana Leaves

Banana leaves make a good weed-blocking layer when establishing lasagna gardens or mulching around perennials. They contain potassium, rot slowly and have long fibers that will tie up your string trimmer if you run it in areas where you've mulched with banana leaves. Chopped banana leaves and stems can be also be used as mulch in annual gardens.

Biochar

Biochar is the remains of burned wood, extinguished in the charcoal stage before burning away into ashes. It has an incredible capacity to absorb minerals. Experiments using it as a long-term amendment and replacement for humus in the soil are ongoing. If you put it in your compost pile or "charge" it first in a nutrient solution, it is reputed to act as a slow-release fertilizer. It also alleged that biochar provides habitat for useful bacteria and fungi in the soil. If you add fresh charcoal to garden beds, however, your plants may starve as the char soaks up all the nutrition it can grab. Steven

Edholm (Skillcult.com) has seen excellent results in the second year after application, as well as subsequent years. Crushed biochar may be a way to improve your sand for a generation or more. It is worth experimenting.

Blood Meal

Blood meal is a quick source of nitrogen for your plants. It is made from dried blood and is a slaughterhouse byproduct. Apply sparingly as a side-dress or you may burn your plants.

Bone Meal

Bone meal is another slaughterhouse by-product, containing phosphorus, calcium, and some micronutrients. It is usually not needed in Florida as our sand tends to contain plenty of phosphorus already.

Borax

Borax supplies boron, a necessary micronutrient that plants crave. It will kill plants if you give them more than a tiny amount, so be careful. A tablespoon carefully dusted over an entire 4' x 8' bed is plenty. It's probably safer to mix it thoroughly with a few gallons of compost, then spread that.

Cardboard

Cardboard is a good weed block. Torn up, it is good source of carbon for your compost pile. Avoid glossy cardboard and stick to the brown stuff. People sometimes ask me if I worry about the glues in it. No, I don't. I figure there are so many toxic things being dumped on us daily that cardboard toxicity is the least of my worries.

Chemical Fertilizers

Bagged chemical fertilizers work quickly in the garden but also wash right through the soil, wasting much of what you add to your beds. If you want to use chemical fertilizers, look for "balanced" ones like 6-6-6 or 10-10-10, or if you have plenty of phosphorus in your soil (your local ag extension can probably tell you), buy 6-0-6 or 10-0-10, etc. Chemical fertilizers are not good for soil life and do not provide the benefits of compost, so I recommend using them if need be, but adding compost along with it if you have it. That said, it's better to grow food with chemical fertilizer than grow nothing because you can't do it all "organically". Food is your primary goal.

Avoid "weed and feed" products because they will kill your gardens. High-nitrogen turf fertilizers that do not contain herbicides can feed very hungry grass crops like corn and sugarcane but are not good for most garden vegetables as they encourage rampant leaf growth rather than fruit and root production.

Though I do not use much bagged fertilizer, I do sometimes feed with crystal liquid fertilizers that contain micronutrients. They provide nutrients quickly and help plants push through drought. I buy an off-brand type that works well and use it as needed. Some might question this choice and declare me an organic heretic, but in my research I have discovered a great irony that pushed me from total organic and back into the use of some chemicals. The irony is that many so-called "organic" amendments contain toxins such as herbicides, antibiotics, medications, heavy metals, pesticides, and more. When a load of manure killed a large amount of my plants due to contamination with Grazon herbicide, I started digging into the safety of various "organic" amendments. And I've kept digging. Some chicken feeds have contained arsenic. Purchased compost may contain biosolids from sewage waste, which in turn contains a wide range of contaminants. Hay and straw often have herbicide and pesticide residue. It's ridiculous! The entire chain of organic amendments is compromised. I now trust little blue crystals from a lab more than I trust manure from a local farmer. How messed up is that? It is the nature of our world at this point, and not something I see changing any time soon. Plants need nutrition, so we just have to make the best choices we can with the information we have. If some inorganic products appear safer, I will use them. Again, the end goal is food. Just make sure you provide micronutrients along with your macros (NPK).

Chicken Manure

Fresh chicken manure is loaded with nitrogen and will roast your plants unless applied very moderately, but composted chicken manure is a great kick-start to a garden bed. Let it rot down in a pile for a few months, then fork a few shovelfuls into a 4' x 8' bed. Along with nitrogen, chicken manure also contains good amounts of phosphorus and potassium.

Clay

In sandy soils, adding some clay to your beds might be a good idea. As I wrote above, I add clay to my compost piles in order to make the humus stick. Baseball diamond clay, bentonite clay, clay you dig in a friend's yard, or clay you bring back from your family vacation to Appalachia—all good to add! Even a bit of pottery clay dust added to the compost pile will work. Clay has a much higher ability to hold onto nutrients than sand does.

Coconut Husks

When wet, coconut husks stay soaked. I bury them at the bottom of container gardens or let them rot in wet piles for a year or more to use in potting mixes.

Coffee Grounds

Used coffee grounds provide nitrogen and a range of micronutrients. You can add them to your compost heap to give it a kickstart or sprinkle them directly on beds and around perennials. Roses love a cup of used grounds and a half cup of Epsom salts a couple times per year, sprinkled around the root base. My friend Cathy does that and gets great results. If it works on roses, it will work on a lot of other plants.

Comfrey Leaves

Comfrey is loved by permaculture enthusiasts and herbalists, but some types do not thrive in Florida. I used it in Tennessee where it grew with gusto, then tried it in Florida and had to fight to keep it alive. The leaves are mineral-rich and can be chopped and used as mulch or put into buckets with water and allowed to rot down into a very good tea for your plants. Though I gave up on it a few years ago, I now have new data. When I hosted an event in The Great South Florida Food Forest Project, one of the attendees shared some huge comfrey plants he had grown in Florida. It was a different variety from what I had tried (Bocking 14), and he told me it was thriving on his homestead. If you can find a type like that, grow it.

Compost

There are so many wondrous things about compost and so many ways to make it that I wrote an entire book on the topic. It is the Rolls-Royce of garden amendments. A straight-up nutrient analysis of compost looks disappointing compared to commercial fertilizer, but it does so much good in your garden that I cannot overstate its value. It's not in the numbers! Compost does have a good range of nutrients and micronutrients (especially if you compost everything!), but its true value goes beyond the chemical analysis. It helps retain moisture in the soil, increases the soil's ability to exchange nutrients with plants, keeps beds fluffier and it is loaded with a massive range of microbial life, many of which help your plants and bolster their immune systems. It is almost impossible to make enough compost unless you really work at it. We compost all our food waste including meat and bones, plus garden waste, plus cow manure from the neighbor's organically grazing cow (no herbicide contamination possible!), plus bamboo leaves we rake up, plus grass clippings from the road, fallen fruit, and more. We even have a composting toilet so we recycle all our *own* manure into compost. We are still not hitting 100% of the supply I would like, but our gardens are large and we are still working on increasing biomass on the farm to meet our compost needs. If you do not have a compost pile yet, stop reading and go make one.

Composted Stable Bedding

Cows, horses, goats, and other ruminants are often kept on straw or sawdust in their stalls. This material absorbs their waste and is traditionally piled up and composted. Some farms will sell or give it away to you. In the past, this was a great source of fertility for your gardens, containing everything vegetables need to thrive. Now, however, most animals are fed with hay that contains herbicide residue capable of passing through their digestion, into the manure, and then into your gardens, destroying them. If you don't believe me, go watch Scott Head's story on YouTube. He's just one of many gardeners that had their plots wrecked by the evils of Big Ag. Avoid.

Cottonseed Meal

I first used cottonseed meal after hearing about it from Steve Solomon. It's one of the ingredients in his "Complete Organic Fertilizer" recipe. We made COF one year and added it to a cabbage bed in fall, then planted cabbages. They were excellent—best I've ever grown. Cottonseed meal is rich in nitrogen and releases it slowly as the soil life digests the meal and makes it available. Unfortunately, cottonseed meal is likely created from GMO cotton and also contains pesticide residue. Use if you like. It works wonderfully but is a bit iffy.

Cow Manure

The best manure you should no longer use in your garden due to persistent herbicide contamination in hay and pasture grass. Thanks, Dow Agro-Sciences. Avoid.

Crab Meal

Allegedly great for gardens and an excellent source of calcium. I have not used it as I've never been able to find it, but I did put a bunch of dead crabs into a big batch of DFSW once.

Cypress Mulch

Cypress mulch is commonly sold in Florida. It's long-lasting and looks nice in landscaping. I wouldn't use it in the garden as it breaks down slowly and doesn't feed your plants enough. And it's expensive.

Dave's Fetid Swamp Water (DFSW)

Note: See how to make this anaerobic compost tea in the above section on foliar feeding.

The wider range of ingredients you can add to this tea, the better. I have dumped almost everything in these mixes, including rotten fruit, weeds, seaweed, urine, kitchen scraps, grass, fish guts, eggshells, Epsom salt, a little Borax, a bucket of seawater, cow bones, and more. It just sits and rots and when you water with it, you give your gardens a good range of quick micronutrients.

Dead Enemies

Compost your enemies and they can feed your soil for years. Bury deeply and plant over the top, or add them to massive compost piles. Fatter enemies may take longer to break down. Remember that vegan enemies are not as nutritious for the garden as meat-eating enemies.

Dog Food

The late great Florida gardener John Starnes shared his method of burying dog food in new garden beds and inside holes on which he then planted yams. As dogs are meat-eaters, their food is formulated with very high protein, which breaks down into nitrogen. I used it a year ago and a stray dog showed up and walked all over my garden eating it. Probably better to bury it deeper unless you have a fence.

Dog Manure

Though dog manure is commonly panned as a garden amendment, it is loaded with nitrogen and a range of other nutrients. Compost it in a hot pile to destroy pathogens or simply bury it in the ground and plant over the top.

Eggshells

Eggshells can be saved and crushed or powdered as a calcium-rich fertilizer. Some gardeners put a handful of them in tomato planting holes to fend off blossom end rot. We just throw our eggshells into the compost pile.

Epsom Salts

Epsom salt is an excellent and fast fertilizer that provides the vital micronutrients magnesium and sulphur. Dissolve a cup of it in a watering can and use that to water unhappy plants. They'll green right up, as magnesium helps plants photosynthesize effectively. You can also add a tablespoon around the base of plants now and again. Note: if you have clay, magnesium will make it bind up tighter and be harder to dig, so keep that in mind. In sand this is not an issue. Note that Epsom Salts is not the same as table salt. The former is magnesium sulfate, which is fine in goodly amounts, the latter is sodium chloride and will burn your plants quickly.

Fish Fertilizer

Fish emulsions and fish fertilizers are excellent tonics for your plants, providing a variety of nutrients that make plants happy. Think of how many minerals are in the sea—fish contain many of them, and are great for the garden. If you do not want to buy fish fertilizer, it is easy to make. Just throw some fish scraps in a bucket and top them off with water, then wait a month or so for it to rot down. Strain and dilute with some water, then water your plants. I have not worked out a standard dilution ratio as the amount of fish material to water varies from batch to batch and I don't bother figuring out exact measurements. When I use it, I usually just add a quart of homemade fish tea to a two-gallon watering can. Purchased fish emulsions and fertilizers are more concentrated, so follow the instructions on the label. It stinks to high heaven but makes plants happy. Leaves get glossy and deep green and fruits increase. I often add fish guts or scraps to my barrels of DFSW. A final note on fish: you know the method you read about in school, where the Indians taught the Pilgrims to bury fish at the bottom of their corn plants? It works like a charm with every plant. You just have to bury your fish or fish scraps deep enough that animals won't dig it up.

Goat Manure

A great garden amendment, but often unsafe due to goats being fed hay from farms that spray Grazon herbicide. Avoid, unless you are raising your own goats on your own grass and not feeding them purchased hay. Feeding them alfalfa and sweet feed should be fine, just avoid hay!

Grass Clippings

If you do not treat your grass with Weed & Feed or ChemDeath or whatever people spray on their lawns, grass clippings are a good garden mulch as well as an excellent "green" addition to your compost piles. When adding them to your garden, it may help to let them dry out a bit on your driveway first and fluff them up some when mulching so they don't get too matted and prevent water from reaching the soil.

Greensand

Greensand is a mined amendment that contains potassium as well as silica, iron and a wide range of other slow-release minerals. It's a good way to increase the nutrient density of your food and also holds sandy soils together.

Gypsum

Gypsum is a good source of calcium that does not mess with your soil's pH like lime does. It loosens clay soil, but it is probably not that useful in sand due to how fast it leaches through.

Horse Manure

Horse manure is weedy and seedy and often contains herbicide. Avoid, unless it is your own horse and you do not buy any hay. In that case, compost the manure, then add to gardens.

Human Hair

I would not get hair from a barber shop as I have no idea what people are spraying on their heads and what else is mixed in with it, but using hair from your family is fine. There's not usually enough to make a difference in your gardens, but I have added it to potted plants and to my compost piles. It's a slow-release nitrogen source.

Humanure

Humanure freaks people out and for good reason. Improper management of sewage causes serious problems with disease in less developed nations. However, we have used Joseph Jenkins' style bucket and sawdust humanure composting toilets off and on for years and never had any issues. Hot composting in a heap deals with pathogens and turns "waste" into valuable compost. It also "closes the nutrient loop," as permaculturists like to say. You eat from your garden and your body uses what it can, then disposes of the rest. You compost that, then add it back into your gardens (or just around your fruit trees, if you are nervous), then your plants reuse the nutrients and feed you again. It's a loop! If you flush away all the manure in your household, you lose all that potential soil fertility. After a year or two of composting, humanure is perfectly safe and contains a wide range of nutrients. Alternatively, just bury fresh buckets of it in the ground and plant over the top. Pumpkins love it.

Kelp Meal

Kelp meal is a micronutrient powerhouse, bringing as many as 70 different minerals with it. It's expensive but worth the price. Add a dusting to new garden beds and your plants will be happy. On a down note, kelp harvested from the Pacific may now be contaminated by radioactive elements discharged in the Fukushima reactor disaster. I do not use Pacific kelp anymore.

Leaf Mould

Leaf mould is compost made from leaves. You can often dig and sift it from forests, or make your own by cold composting big piles of leaves. It takes a couple years to make but is good stuff and filled with beneficial fungi. Perennials and fruit trees appreciate it.

Leguminous Tree Leaves

There are many trees in the bean and pea family that have beneficial relationships with soil bacteria that take atmospheric nitrogen and convert it into a form plants can use. These scrappy trees use the nitrogen for growth and often have leaves that are rich in it. In Central and North Florida, black locust, cassias, mimosa and *Leucaena leucocephala* (a common "weed" tree) are excellent "chop-and-drop" plants, meaning you can just chop up their leaves and branches and drop them at the base of plants you wish to feed. My daughter often gathers nitrogen-fixer leaves and spreads them around her garden beds as a thin mulch to feed her vegetables and flowers. In South Florida, there are many more leguminous species to use including ear-pod tree, necklace pod, Pride of Barbados (also called dwarf poinciana), royal poinciana, and more. If it has feathery leaves and bears pods that look like beans or peas, it's probably a nitrogen-fixer and high in nitrogen.

The leaves can also be added to DFSW or fermented down by themselves as a nitrogen source. I add them to compost piles, use them as part of my mulching regime, and let them grow all over my food forest projects where they get cut again and again for mulch. Don't cut them down and kill them, just crop them back multiple times a year and use the trimmings as fertilizer and mulch for other plants.

Lime (Ag)

A good source of calcium. Don't add too much as it can raise the pH of your soil beyond what plants like. If you have acid soils, a little lime will help. If you are planning to use lime, it's a good idea to test your soil's pH first to make sure you don't over-lime and raise the pH beyond what your plants like. Over-liming can wreck a garden for a year or more.

Lime (Dolomitic)

Another source of calcium made from crushed limestone. The same pH warnings apply.

Milorganite

Milorganite is made of treated Milwaukee sewage. When I was a kid, dad used it on our lawn and it made the grass very happy. Though I believe in recycling waste as much as we can, using biosolids like Milorganite is not good for gardens because of its contaminants, including arsenic and other heavy metals. I wouldn't put it on my lawn, either. Dad didn't know the risks back then, but we do now. Avoid.

Moringa

Moringa is a fast-growing tropical tree with a wide range of health benefits. As a chop-and-drop, it is a great fertilizer. Studies have shown that when used as a fertilizer, moringa stimulates plant growth. High in nitrogen and a wide range of micronutrients, as moringa is a very effective nutrient accumulator.

Oak Leaves

Oak leaves take a long time to rot and are best for slow leaf mould compost piles or as mulch around perennials.

Oyster Shell

Oyster shell is a good slow-release calcium source. I buy the shell sold for chickens and scatter it in my beds.

Palm Fronds

Palm fronds break down slowly and are not good in compost piles, but they are a decent mulch. Chop them into pieces or just lay entire fronds on the ground. I've used them as a weed block with decent effectiveness. They are good as the bottom layer of lasagna gardens and for stuffing in the bottom of container gardens. Palm fronds are also nice to use as shade over new transplants on hot days. You can often prop the fronds up a little bit over the transplants so they don't crush them, allowing in some dappled light. In a couple of days when the transplants have rooted in well, remove the fronds. Palm fronds can also be woven into a wide range of useful things, including little mats you can place beneath developing melons to keep them off the ground and safer from rot.

Paper (Shredded)

Shredded paper from your home or office can be added to compost piles as a carbon layer or used as a decent, though trashy looking, mulch. It's almost all carbon. I have done some reading on the toxicity of printer inks and they don't seem to be a big deal.

Peanut Hay

Peanut hay is a great high-nitrogen material for feeding beds. Used as mulch, it rots quickly and releases nutrients into the soil. It's also a good green addition to your compost.

Peat Moss

Peat moss is useful in potting mixes, but I do not bother adding it to garden beds. It tends to dry up and disappear or become hydrophobic and resist water.

Pine Bark Mulch

This is good for blueberries and other acid-loving perennials but too expensive to be good in the garden, as well as not breaking down in a reasonable timeframe.

Pine Needles

Similar to pine back mulch, pine needles are loved by blueberries, etc. I have used it as a garden mulch as well, but it is better for keeping in soil moisture than for building soil.

Rabbit Manure

Rabbit manure is an excellent fertilizer and usually is not contaminated with Aminopyralid herbicide, unless the rabbits are bedded in hay or straw. It has a good range of nutrients and can be added on top of garden beds and in containers as a slow-release fertilizer. When we kept rabbits I used the manure in my nursery plants and gardens and was quite glad for it.

Rock Dust

Various rock dusts contain a range of minerals that many gardeners swear by. It's a slow-release way to increase nutrition in the soil.

Sawdust

Sawdust is very high in carbon and takes a long time to break down unless mixed with nitrogenous materials. Tilling it into a garden will suck up the soil's nitrogen reserves. It can be added in moderation to compost piles. It really works well in a composting toilet system.

Sea Salt

The ocean contains an abundance of minerals and I believe a little sea salt in the garden is a good thing. My preferred way to get it is to bring home ocean water and pour some in my DFSW barrel. Though the salt in seawater will burn plants, in small amounts it really improves the flavor of some crops, especially tomatoes. Sea salt is a good amendment for coconut palms, increasing their vigor and yields. You can just carry home buckets of seawater and dump it at the base of coconut palms, just be careful not to soak less salt-tolerant plants around them.

Seaweed

For years I have gathered seaweed on the beach and thrown it into my compost piles, used it as mulch and tossed it into DFSW. I do not rinse it when mulching tomatoes, but I have had unwashed seaweed mulch burn other plants. I do not bother rinsing it before adding it to compost piles and have not had any issues. A little salt in the garden is good. But just a little! Seaweed contains a wide range of minerals and is generally a great amendment unless it has arrived after drifting through an area where there is a lot of runoff. Some islands in the Caribbean have lots of pesticide and other toxic runoffs going into the ocean, which is accumulated by passing seaweed and then ends up on beaches far away. If you add this to your gardens, you can end up with toxins and heavy metals along with your micronutrients. I don't pick up as much seaweed in my area now that I know this issue.

Spanish Moss

Spanish moss is a good mulch and a good addition to compost piles. Despite hearing dire warnings about its ability to hold chiggers, it has never given me a single itch in years of my using it in the garden.

Straw and Hay

I do not recommend either straw or hay due to the possibility of herbicide contamination, unless you can get them from a known organic source. This is also why I stay away from straw bale gardening.

Urea

Urea is a nitrogen fertilizer that is very strong. So strong that it will burn plants, especially if added to seed or transplant holes. If you use it, mix it into the soil well, then plant, or use as a side-dressing a little ways from plant stems. If it sits on top of the ground, it degrades fast, so it is better to cover it.

Urine

Urine is a readily available high nitrogen fertilizer you can make at home in your spare time. Dilute it six parts water to one part urine for most plants. Corn and bananas take it straight without complaining. Too much urine in one place can burn plants, especially if you have a high-salt diet. Urine also contains a variety of micronutrients. It doesn't seem to matter if you use it fresh or aged. I store it in old 750ml bottles, then pour one of those into my two-gallon watering can, fill the rest with water, then water the gardens. Sandy gardens really, really appreciate being watered with urine.

Every time I mention it's a safe fertilizer, people always comment with something like "But what if you take 16 medications? Is it still safe?" No, it's probably not. But neither is taking most medications. If you're using it on your own garden, it's probably not going to hurt you. Still, most of us don't want Zoloft and Oxycontin in our tomatoes. My advice is to get off the meds, if you can, man. Yeah, man. Stay away from drugs.

Water Hyacinth

Water hyacinth is a prolific invasive aquatic plant that costs the state of Florida millions every year. It's a biomass machine, reproducing at an incredible rate and choking up waterways. It's also a great fertilizer for your gardens.

Once removed from the water, the plant dies and rapidly rots down into the ground, releasing water and a range of nutrients. It's worth growing in ponds (kept far from any waterways!) just to add to your gardens and compost piles. Throwing it around the base of fruit trees provides both water and nutrients to the trees. Great stuff.

Weeds

When weeds grow all over your yard and garden, be happy! God designed them to cover bare soil and create humus. Harvest them and feed them to your plants. Weeds can be scythed or sickled down and used as mulch around trees and shrubs, added to DFSW, and thrown in your compost pile. It's best to avoid letting them go to seed, but if they do I use them as mulch around trees and not in my compost or compost tea. Some weeds

Water hyacinth: Florida's worst aquatic invasive makes great compost.

fix nitrogen, some accumulate phosphorus, others are good at pulling up micronutrients and yet others have some of everything. A mix of weeds is a good food for other plants. Remember that weeds are hardy, pioneer species that are usually great at thriving under adverse conditions thanks to their ability to gather what they need from the ground. Let them grow a bit, then harvest their hard work and feed it to your food plants.

Wood Chips

Tree companies clear brush and trees all the time and shred it up. If you're lucky, you can catch a truck and have them dump a pile of mulch in your yard. I do not grow my vegetable gardens in tree mulch as I find it hard to weed around and painful to use in a large garden. Hauling mulch and getting it thick enough to keep down Florida weeds is a wearisome task. In my food forests and around trees, however, I love to put down plenty of mulch. The year after I dropped it in my North Florida food forest, all my fruit trees grew rapidly and really started being happy. Before, they had just been in sand. The soil under mulch is filled with loamy humus after a few months pass and it just gets better after a year or more. Tree company mulch is better than cypress or pine bark or other single-species mulches, as it's cut green and usually contains a range of shredded-up tree and plant species. Everything from oak branches to palm fronds and pine and poincianas end up in it, and all of them contain different balances of nutrients. Pile them together still green, and they start composting together. I let a large load of mulch rot down for over a year once and it turned into nice, loamy humus with some rotten wood pieces still in it. I mixed it half-and-half with purchased potting soil and filled nursery pots with it—the plants were quite happy! Wood chips are high in carbon and should not be used fresh either in pots or tilled into your gardens since they'll bind up nitrogen and starve plant roots until they rot down.

Watering

I have watered in a variety of ways over the years. We've used drip irrigation, watered by hose, by lawn sprinkler, and then eventually put up PVC stand pipes over the garden and watered from our well. That was by far the easiest method.

I find drip irrigation to be an utter pain in the neck. The tubing is a pain to weed around with a hoe and often clogs or leaks or both. I do not enjoy running pipes through the garden and I don't like the way it looks, either. I've also discovered that squirrels like to chew into soaker hoses to get water. You may enjoy plumbing—and if so, this method may work fine for you—but I much prefer overhead irrigation with a few "rain bird" sprinkler heads on stand pipes, with PVC supply lines buried underground. It can be set up in a weekend if you have a handy friend. Allan the Beekeeper and I did my irrigation setup in a day and it worked great. Once it was done, my wife could water the garden by turning a valve, setting a timer, then turning it off afterwards. We shoot to give our gardens an inch of water a couple days per week. If you put an empty cup or container in an open area of your garden and run your sprinklers, you can time out how long it takes to fill the cup one inch, then you know how long to run your sprinkler system.

Some people say that drip irrigation is better for plants, but I think they enjoy the rain from above, with the possible exception of tomatoes. If you are growing tomatoes or other plants susceptible to mildews and bacteria issues, such as summer squash, then I recommend watering your garden in the early morning rather than in the evening. Generally I just water when they look thirsty.

Water deeply. An inch is good. Watering shallowly is not good for plant root development and encourages shallow root systems near the surface. It is much better to water deeply and less often than to water shallowly every day. If you get a good rainfall, you can go without watering for a few days. You can wait even longer if your gardens have wider spacing.

Wide garden spacing allows each plant to have more space to find what they need beneath the soil. Biointensive methods encourage very tight spacing for maximum production, and they require more watering because of it. A tightly spaced bed often needs daily watering and very high fertility to be productive as crowded plants fight beneath the soil for limited nutrient and water reserves. I prefer to space my crops a little wider so they can go a little longer without water. If you have a very tight backyard, close garden spacing might be better for you, but if you have a little more space, your crops will be happy to have some breathing room. I plant unirrigated corn in stations 4' apart or in rows 3' apart. If I planted them at 18" apart, I would have to run water on them regularly. At wider spacing, they usually do decently just on rainfall.

The quality of your water also matters. If you can pump from a river, canal or lake (and the water is not brackish), it's better for your garden than chlorinated city water. Rainwater or well water is also better. Yields decrease when plants are given chlorinated water. It will keep them alive, but they don't like it. That's why my plants only drink pure grain alcohol and distilled water. Anything else would dilute their essence.

I am kidding. The alcohol is for Rachel and me. And distilled water is not as good for your plants as rain, well or lake/river/canal water.

If you have a small garden, you can water with a hose or watering cans. It's time consuming but enjoyable work that gives you a good chance to see every plant as you water. Catching rainwater is a very good idea. If you can buy a big water tank—1,000 gallons is great—and run your gutters into it, you have a much better source of water than your municipal supply. Put it on a raised platform and you'll have pressure enough to water your beds. On our current property we have a 600 gallon tank I recently installed next to a little cabin. It's uphill from our gardens but not quite high enough to let us have great pressure when I run a hose down. Instead of slowly watering everything directly from the tank, I have a 55-gallon drum with an open top sitting by the garden. We run the hose down to it and fill it with rainwater from the big tank, then dip into that 55-gallon tank with watering cans to water the rows. It helps to have a kid filling cans and walking the full ones to you in the garden and taking the empties back to be filled in the drum. Dipping into an open tank is much faster than filling each can from a trickling hose.

On my old property in North Florida, I put three old 300-gallon hot tubs in my gardens and filled them with the hose. In summer, the rains would keep the water levels high. Then I put in some fish to eat mosquitoes and added pond plants to the top. The pond plants were harvested as mulch and compost when they covered the entire surface. I'd take about half of them and let them grow back again. The water I would use to water anything that really needed it. If a tree in a pot dried out, I would soak it in the pond. If I wanted a quick place to dip a watering can, the hot tub pond was there. They also served as an emergency water supply in case the power went out for an extended period of time and I could no longer run my well.

Plants that are well-fed need less water than those that are starving. "Fertigating", that is, irrigating with a weak fertilizer solution, is a very good way to perk plants up and keep them strong. This is where your barrel of swamp water is handy, though we also water with soluble non-organic balanced fertilizers which also contain micronutrients. Dip into your stinky bucket of DFSW with a watering can and feed in the morning or evening every week or two and it will help keep plants happy.

Mulching will increase the ability of the ground to hold water. Tending plants well and getting them to fill out quickly and shade the ground also helps. The sun is very hot during the middle of the day in Florida and bare ground can burn your feet as well as plant roots.

Some people swear by hugelkultur gardening as a way to keep moisture in the ground. With a hugelkultur garden, logs and sticks are piled in a mound, then soil is piled on top of them, then the pile is planted. Over time, the woody material rots and soaks up moisture and becomes a reservoir for plant roots. I've seen mixed results in Florida, as our sand drains very fast and does not mound over a pile of wood very well, so the hugelkultur mounds I saw were a dry mess of sticks and sand. Personally, the most hugelkultur I've done is burying the occasional mess of rotten wood at the bottom of a container (I did this in tire gardens and in an old fridge) or a melon pit, then planting over it, so I cannot definitively claim the method does not work. If you try it and get great results, please send pictures and let me know. At any rate, it's not a good Florida survival gardening strategy for a larger garden as it takes a huge mess of wood and a lot more time to build each bed.

Over years of experimenting, my favorite method is to dig beds and give them some compost, then water with stand pipes and do some mulching as I have materials. If I don't, I don't worry about it and I just plant the bare ground, then feed with what I have.

Chapter 6

TOOLS

As anyone who subscribes to my YouTube channel knows, we use all hand tools on our farm, with the notable exception of a Stihl string trimmer for cutting paths and grass. On my previous property I often cut grass with an antique scythe, but our current homestead has a lot of blade-destroying rocks so I stick with my trimmer.

There are a few reasons for this Luddite approach to gardening. First, I don't like having to fix and maintain machines. Second, I don't like spending money on expensive tools. Third, we only farm a half-acre, so getting a chainsaw, or a tiller, or a tractor is not needed. Fourth, I simply enjoy using good hand tools that work with a little human power. Fifth, it's good exercise, and I need exercise so I don't end up looking like the average writer.

Unfortunately, it's getting hard to find decent tools, even simple hand tools. Modern garden tools are mostly junk. Somewhere along the line, the good stuff was stolen from us.

Did you ever hold an old silver dollar in your hand? Or, even better, a gold coin? A hundred years ago, our money was real. Tangible. Beautiful and well-made. Now the nations of the world have replaced precious metals with paper, aluminum, steel, and other base metals. The US penny isn't even made from solid copper anymore! It also won't buy you a piece of candy, like its ancestors, because its real value has been inflated away and stolen. It's a zinc slug, coated with a shiny copper coating that turns green and corrodes faster than you can say "Federal Reserve." It may look like a copper penny, but it's not. And you certainly can't trade 100 pennies for a chunky silver dollar. It's junk that looks like it isn't.

Garden tools have suffered in a similar manner. When you buy a spading fork from your local hardware store, it may look similar to your grandpa's fork. It might even look nicer. Yet when you take it home and put it to work, you'll rapidly find you've been sold something that looks like a fork but is instead a piece of bendy junk. Forget trying to break new ground with it. You almost have to do all your digging first, then only use your fork to loosen already loose soil. What's the use in that?

The ordinary garden hoe has suffered a similar fate. What you'll find now is a cheap blade, welded onto a cheap swan's neck that fits into the hole in a wooden handle and is held in place by a cheap collar. It doesn't hold a good edge and after some use, you often can't keep the head on the handle. It's a poor imitation of the hoes of the past, which were all one piece of good steel. The blade and the swan's neck and the collar on an old hoe were all one piece. The collar fit over the end of a tapered wooden handle and was held in tightly by a small nail or screw or two that went through the steel into the handle. It was easy to repair if the handle gave up on you, plus the steel would take a great edge and stay sharp through the decapitation of untold weeds. An antique hoe is a joy to use, and its head isn't going to fall off.

The modern hoe head on the left is made from three pieces of cheap metal, the quality antique hoe on the right is made of one piece of good steel.

You should not have to baby your gardening tools. Tools should be able to work as hard as you do, or harder.

Now we're stuck with junk. Maybe as we sink into a new Great Depression and gardening takes off, people will quit buying from China and start producing some good tools again right here in Florida. Maybe you'll be the one. Now there's a thought! .

Enough dreaming. Let's run down the basic tools you need for a garden, starting with the tools you should have, then moving on to a list of tools that are nice to have.

Tools You Should Have

Spade/Shovel

In order to cut sod and turn the soil, a spade or a shovel is a must-have tool. Spades should have a thin springy blade that has been sharpened to a knife-like edge. A sharp blade makes digging (relatively) easy. An honestly manufactured blade stays sharp, though the blade will be entirely blunt when the tool is purchased. A 15-degree blade angle is fine for sand and will save you some effort, as well as cutting grass and rooting like a boss. I do have a thick-bladed spade I've used for double-digging beds, but it's tiring to use. Recently I got an old thin-bladed, almost square-pointed spade that is lighter and works great in sand.

Shovels and spades come with either short or long handles. Short handles are generally more tiring to use than long handles.

Hoe

After a shovel/spade, the next most important tool is a hoe.

Grasses and broad leaved weeds thrive in unirrigated infertile soil; they withstand extreme competition and still reproduce. Vegetables once were edible wild plants before humans redesigned them to provide larger amounts of better tasting food at the cost of becoming far less competitive. Vegetables require fertile, moist soil and minimal competition. If weeds are allowed to come up and grow at the same time the vegetables start out they soon suppress the vegetables. There is no way around it! A few weeds that come up after your vegetables and don't grow tall enough to shade them won't do much harm to that crop—but if you let them make seeds, you'll have more weeds to deal with later. If you hoe regularly and knock down the weeds, you'll have less and less weeding to deal with in future gardens.

Many garden writers recommend jamming plants so close together they must be weeded by hand as you crouch over the beds or squat in the path. The supposed benefit is more food from less area, yet intensive arrangements require meticulous hand work and are time consuming. If you have enough land to spread plants out it is worth the savings in effort. Weeding with a hoe is easier than constant hand weeding. No matter which gardening style is used, you won't take a ton of time weeding if you're only taking care of a few 4' x 8' beds, but if your goal is to produce a diverse year-round abundance that covers dinner plates every day of the year then the garden must be large. Hand weeding that many beds takes too many hours and is incredibly tedious.

Better to give your plants plenty of growing room and eliminate weeds with a hoe. A large garden takes up more space, but it's easily manageable if you can hoe rather than hand-weed. The spacings I suggest in this book give you enough space between plants that you can easily weed them with a hoe when they are young. Later, the leaf canopy shades the ground enough to suppress weeds and you can quit all the hoeing. The rare weed that does get above your crops is easily tugged out.

Hoeing young weeds goes quickly and takes little effort if blade is sharp and the surface is loose. Hoeing once a week insures that no weed makes seed and makes the next year's hoeing easier. A recently hoed surface is always easy to work the next time as every weed will still be small. Done this way it takes no more effort to hoe the aisles and paths than it does to sweep a floor. If your weeds are allowed to grow on for another full week, it gets harder to clean up your beds. Wait three weeks and you're in trouble, especially during Florida's rainy season. Knock them down when they're small and it's an easy job.

The key to success is a sharp hoe. A weeding hoe should work like a knife that severs a small plant's main stem just below the surface. Boom! Dead! Hoeing little weeds does not use a lot of energy. In order to work efficiently the hoe's blade must sit flat on the soil's surface as you stand up straight and hold the handle. The blade should slice through the soil just below the surface. If your hoe blade is angled downward it tends to bury itself deeper and you end up dragging dirt. If the blade is angled upward, it tends to lift itself out of the soil. Then the hoer bends over to compensate which unnecessarily tires the back. That's why the blade attaches to the handle with a rod of mild bendable steel (called a swansneck) so that the blade's angle of attack can be adjusted to match the user's height and natural stance. Bending the swansneck is best done by resting it against the corner of an anvil and tapping it firmly with a hammer. Don't try to bend it very much in one go. It usually takes but the slightest tweak (done a few times) to get it perfect.

The common garden hoe will be entirely blunt when you buy it. Working with a blunt hoe is about as exhausting and ineffective as trying to sharpen a blunt hoe for the first time with a dull file. Buy a new one if yours are old or rusty. Clamp the blade in a bench vice and patiently grind down the outside face until no more than a 15° bevel is formed—like a wood chisel.

If you don't have a workbench, brace the hoe somewhere tightly and start filing. Get the bevel perfect, then remove the very thin metal burr that filing on one side has pushed over the edge. Do this by giving the opposite face a few light strokes with the file pressed flat against the blade to avoid grinding even the slightest bevel into that side. With the burr removed, a 15° chisel-like edge should almost cut your finger if you press hard. Filing an effective edge for the first time takes work. It's important to hold the file at exactly the same angle through each and every stroke or else the bevel will never get sharp. And don't take what may seem to be the easy way out by making the bevel less acute (and less sharp) so that there's less metal to grind off—that only makes weeding many times harder than any effort saved when filing.

The common garden hoe is common because its design is so versatile. It slices, scrapes and chops and is good for making seed-planting furrows. If the manufacturer went to the expense of welding the swansneck to a substantial socket that the handle goes into, then the hoe should prove to be unbreakable and the blade should stay sharp. If the swansneck itself is stuck in a hole drilled in the handle, with a thin metal collar wrapped around the outside, then likely the blade is also junk and won't hold an edge. This cheap hoe probably will cost far more in time and effort than the dollars it saved. Cheap steel is quick to shape, easy to weld and won't stay sharp. If filing the initial bevel goes quickly then you're working metal that loses its edge just as quickly. Tool steel and forged steel cost more. Good steel is hard; it takes more time and effort to sharpen the first time but may never need to be resharpened if you're working in sand.

In summer, weeds can get away from you if you aren't out in the garden regularly. Chopping is the only way to get big weeds out. My favorite hoe is an antique I purchased in Micanopy years ago and pressed back into service. The socket, swansneck and blade are all one piece of steel and it cuts through weeds like a hot knife through butter. I've since bought multiple antique hoe heads on ebay and put handles on them for my wife and children to use. They are better than any I've found in the hardware store.

A modern hoe you can find that does work well, however, is the "stirrup" hoe, also known as the "scuffle hoe" or the "hula" hoe. It has a hooped blade that rocks back and forth on a pivot, allowing the gardener to cut weeds on the push and pull strokes. It's great in Florida sand and I highly recommend using one.

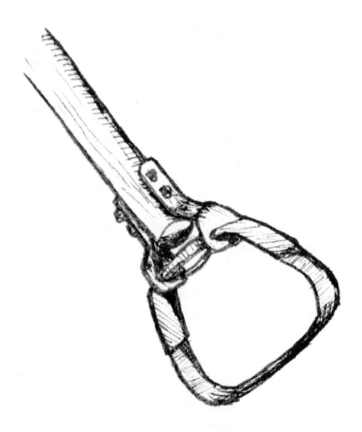

The hula hoe has a blade that rocks back and forth, decapitating weeds on the push and the pull stroke. (Drawing by my eldest son)

Fork

Some years ago I bought a Clarington Forge spading fork with an extra long handle that better fits my height. Back then, they were still made in England, at the same forge where they'd been made for over two hundred years. It is a great fork that turns the ground without bending. I recommended them for a few years, until I heard that the company had shifted its production to India. Now I no longer trust the forks and do not recommend them, despite assurances that they're the same quality they've ever been. I have no faith in third-world standards. I'll bet they wish in the wake of the 2020 pandemic that they'd kept their old forge inside the UK. What a stupid thing to send your productive capacity overseas, especially with something great you've made for centuries.

A good fork is hard to find, but even some of the cheaper ones may stand up to Florida sand. Just look for good, stiff, thick tines. Don't go cheap when you buy a fork, and don't mistake a manure fork/pitchfork for a spading/digging fork. Pitchforks are just for moving hay and straw around, not for digging. Spading forks have four thick tines made to be forced into the soil.

A solid spading fork is an excellent tool for making new garden beds.
(Drawing by my 11-year-old son)

If you find an old spading fork at an antique sale, pick it up. One farmer I met was digging his field and discovered the head of an antique fork in the soil, still in working condition. He put a new handle on it and has been using it ever since. Now that's the way tools should be made!

In light soil a fork can loosen a bed far more quickly than a spade can. Push the tines in all the way, then pull the handle back to loosen the ground. Then pull the fork out, move back a few inches, push it in again and level the handle back again. It's smart to spread compost and other amendments before forking a bed because some of it falls into the momentary openings the fork makes.

Don't push your fork too hard or try to pry up rocks and roots with it, especially if it's a cheapie.

Rakes

It's good to have both a hard-tined rake and a leaf rake. The former is indispensable when you make garden beds, as it allows you to rake out weeds and grass and shape beds. The latter is good for final touches or for gathering up fallen leaves and grass clippings for your compost pile.

Tools that are Nice to Have

Baskets

We bought a variety of baskets from local thrift stores so we could carry in our produce. Large, open ones are good for bulky leaf vegetables like mustard and pak choi and smaller ones are good for picking beans, tomatoes, and other small crops. If you have fruit trees, it's also great to have a large, strong basket or two for gathering oranges, avocados, mangoes, peaches, etc. Buckets will work in a pinch but aren't as pleasant. Or pretty enough for your glitzy Instagram feed.

Broadfork

An American-made tool I trust and recommend, which stands in somewhat for a spading fork, is the Meadow Creature broadfork. I own and use the standard 14" model, which allows me to dig deep beds and till new ground. I've been using it for years without breaking it, though the tips of some of the tines have now turned a little from being plunked down too hard onto rock by a friend who borrowed it from me. The Meadow Creature is a solid steel four-tined, two-handled monster that looks rather like something you'd use to storm the gates of a medieval fortress. The illustration is by my daughter.

To use it, thunk the tines into the ground, then step up on the cross bar and rock it back and forth so the tines work themselves into the ground. Once they've gone as deep as they want to go, you step off and rock the handles back, breaking up the soil above. Then move back a little bit and do

A solid one-piece steel broadfork.
(Drawing by my 14-year-old daughter)

it again. It's like having a giant spading fork. In sand, you can till as much as 10,000 square feet of garden in a day. In clay, you'd be lucky to hit 1,000 square feet in the same time. There are other broadfork manufacturers that make lighter models than the Meadow Creature and those might also work well in Florida sand. I am tough on tools so I stick to the Meadow Creature.

Buckets

Buckets are useful for hauling water and amendments, harvesting, using to make compost tea, and for a variety of home tasks. I tuck yam heads in a five-gallon bucket over winter and store them under the house to keep until spring. We use buckets in our composting outhouse system. We press them into service to store wood ash and homemade fish fertilizer. You can even grow decent vegetables in soil-filled buckets with some holes drilled in the bottom. It's hard to have too many.

Eye Hoes

I have multiple digging or "grub" hoes, also known as "eye hoes" because they have a hole that a handle fits into. Some of them are multi-purpose weeding and digging types and others that are more dedicated to one or the other. I highly recommend them, as they work the soil easier than digging with a shovel. Bring the head down and THUNK!, you've torn a divot from the ground.

One of my favorites for weeding large areas very quickly is the broad-bladed but light "grape hoe" sold by EasyDigging.com. I never want to go without one again. I also like their triangle hoe, which is a very fast weeder of large areas. I've beaten mine to death and need to get another one before too long.

Knife

A sharp little knife is a valuable garden tool. A knife is useful for harvesting, thinning young seedlings and slicing up tomatoes for impromptu taste-tests in the garden.

When a newly-emerged row needs thinning, the slow way to thin is with your fingers. The easy way is by cutting surplus seedlings off just below the soil line with a small, pointed knife that is quite sharp at the tip—like a mini-hoe. Running a knife-sharp blade through soil rapidly dulls it, so keep a stone or file handy. You can also use a pair of scissors for thinning. Author and inventor Herrick Kimball keeps an old mailbox on a post in his garden for storing knives, gloves, scissors, and other bits and pieces out of the rain. I love the idea.

Machete

In Central America, a machete is a farmer's indispensable tool, used for everything from digging to clearing brush to cutting yam poles to slaughtering cows. It's also often used for peeling oranges and opening coconuts while on lunch break. In a Florida garden, the machete is excellent for transplanting and cutting roots, as well as for clearing new ground, chopping material up for a compost pile, harvesting sugarcane and, when used tightly parallel to the soil, for scalping weeds.

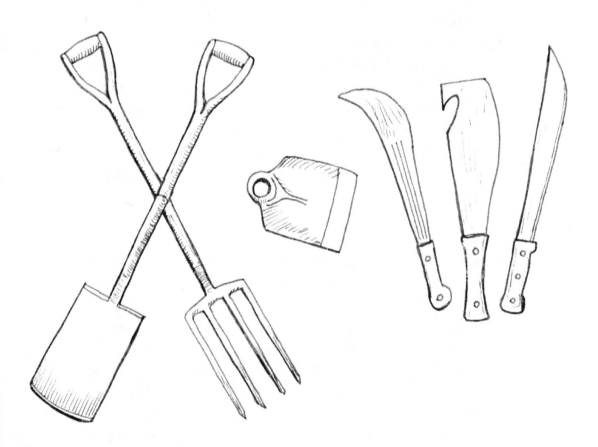

From left to right: Spade, digging fork, eye hoe, Martindale "cutlass" machete, a cane machete, and a Tramontina machete.

If you purchase a machete, most every variety imported from tropical American countries will serve you well. Tramontina and Corona are both good. The English Martindale company also makes excellent machetes that are used across the Caribbean. They differ somewhat from their Spanish-speaking cousins in having slightly thicker blades that are less springy. Buy a machete that fits your hand well and isn't too heavy. There are quite heavy models that can make short work of thick brush but will also tire the hand rapidly. I prefer a shorter, cutlass-style Martindale machete for most work, as it isn't heavy and is easy to control, though I recently bought one of my sons a short-bladed Tramontina and am very impressed with how fast it works and how it holds an edge.

When picking fruit or working with grasses, sugarcane or pulling vines, a "cane knife" style machete with a hook on the back is nice to have, as the hook is quite useful for catching material and pulling it close to be chopped. Cane machetes are not good for transplanting or stabbing as the end is blunt. Just be careful with cane machetes. I once cut through two tendons in the back of my left hand with one while attempting to open a coconut. I was wearing a wide-brimmed straw hat and as I brought the blade down, the hook on the back caught the edge of my hat, misdirecting the blade inwards by a few inches and putting it squarely across the base of my index finger. That was an awful experience we would rather have all of you avoid. A sharp machete is a cold and heartless tool, dividing flesh even more readily than coconut husks.

Scissors

Scissors are great for snipping unwanted seedlings to the ground during thinning. They are also good for quickly chopping up greens for the pot.

Spacing Sticks

One morning, my seven-year-old son and I made a few spacing sticks for our gardens. We made them in 2', 3' and 4' lengths. As the paths are 2' wide and the beds 4', those two sticks were quite useful for establishing new beds. The 3' stick we used for spacing okra and unirrigated corn. Having a few spacing sticks is a quick way to space out your beds and your seeds and transplants. Ours are made from thin lengths of pressure-treated pine, painted white with different colors at the ends of the sticks. I might make myself a 1' and a 6' at some point, but that might just be getting silly. Once you have a few, you can guesstimate the rest. For example, if you wanted to plant beans 2' apart, you could just lay a 4' stick on your bed, then plant a bean at each end and one in the middle. Having a variety of spacing sticks could be silly. Then again, if you aren't too neurotic, you can just use your own body for spacing, using pacing and cubits and palm widths.

Tiller
A tiller is nice to use when you have a big area to till up. A broadfork doesn't require gas and doesn't break, though, so I've quit using tillers and sold the three broken ones that had cluttered up my barn. The only time I miss a tiller is when I'm looking at a big field or chunk of lawn and wish I could just tear it up in a few hours. In that case, it's nice to rent one or have a friend till for you.

Trowel
Who needs a trowel? You have a machete now! Actually, my wife prefers transplanting with a trowel, so I keep one for her.

Watering Can
A watering can is good to have for transplants and for foliar feeding. It's also nice when you just want to water a small area without dragging out the hose.

Wheelbarrow
A wheelbarrow is quite handy when building beds, making compost, hauling soil, and distributing materials. Get a solid one, but not the heavy ones made for concrete, as they are a pain to manage. Having a single wheel is good, as you can navigate in tighter spaces. Most wheelbarrows at the big box shop are junky—don't get the cheapest one. Try to find a good one—or hunt garage sales and get an old one and fix it up.

Wheel Hoe
The wheel hoe is a nice tool for larger gardens, as it allows you to rapidly clear weeds from a path. It's an interesting tool that almost disappeared from the American garden decades ago. Recently, however, it's started to make a comeback thanks to the internet and a lot of small farmers interested in getting maximum output from quality hand tools without resorting to gas-guzzling tillers.

The most famous wheel hoe is the classic Planet Jr. cultivator. Unfortunately, Planet Jr. went out of business years ago, though there's still a thriving trade in their implements on eBay and in the antiques world. A good old Planet Jr. wheel hoe will usually set you back $200 or more. The wheel hoe allows you to clean up a field plot in a fraction of the time it would take you with any other hoe. The wheel in front allows an incredibly efficient distribution of force that works wonders in decapitating weeds, especially when it's teamed up with the oscillating blade behind it, which rocks back and forth depending on if you're pushing or pulling, decapitating weeds both ways.

We own Herrick Kimball's "Planet Whizbang Wheel Hoe", which is a well-designed kit-built wheel hoe. It is monster at clearing weeds. The way

The Planet Whizbang wheel hoe. (Drawing by my 9-year-old son)

the oscillating hoe rocks back and forth as you push/pull the hoe makes it almost possible to cut sod with it. My 9-year-old son likes using our wheel hoe and drew an illustration so you can see what it looks like.

The Planet Whizbang wheel hoe doesn't have any additional attachments, unfortunately. For that, you need to turn to manufactured wheel hoes such as Hoss, Glaser, or Valley Oak, to name a few. There are probably more now, but it's been some time since I was in the market. Hoss also makes a seeder attachment for their wheel hoes, allowing you to plant a large garden in a limited amount of time.

You can get lost in the world of garden tools and implements, yet you really don't need much to build and maintain gardens. A shovel, a fork, a rake, a machete, and a hoe will cover most of the work that needs doing. Don't go chasing gadgets—there's a reason our most common gardening tools have stuck around since antiquity!

Chapter 7

WEEDS

Weeds compete with garden vegetables, consuming water and nutrients and choking out tender plants with their rampant growth. Most of our common vegetables have been selected over millennia for tenderness and flavor and yield, not for their scrappiness. Wild plants will whip garden plants in a street fight. Your job is to keep them from showing up and beating down your crops. In this chapter, we'll cover some various methods of weed control and their pros and cons.

First, though, I must share my appreciation for weeds. They cover the ground, build soil, accumulate nutrients, and some of them are edible. Weeds in your garden are just doing what they were made to do: colonize bare soil and pave the way for shrubs, vines and trees. When you tear up the ground, the soil seed bank is opened and many weeds show up seemingly overnight to fix the damage to the ground. Repeatedly mowing your grass (or patch of weeds, like my "lawn") will keep the ecosystem at a low level of development and stop the succession of plants that leads to woods. Stop mowing, and the annual weeds will be followed by perennial weeds and brush, then pioneer trees and eventually oaks, pines, hickories, or whatever the local geology and climate allows to thrive. The weeds that pop up on cleared ground are just the advance troops of an army of succession that eventually leads to woodland.

As I mention in the chapter on feeding, weeds are a good source of nutrition for the garden and can be composted or added to DSFW to convert their hard work into fuel for your garden.

Just don't let them take over! Here are some weed control methods we've used and some thoughts on each.

Weed Control Methods

Chopping and Dropping

This is one of my favorite ways to knock down and re-use weeds in my food forests, around perennials, and sometimes in the vegetable garden. I learned the concept from Geoff Lawton long ago in his film *Establishing a Food Forest the Permaculture Way*. Any weeds and unwanted brush or trees can be chopped down and spread as mulch around the base of trees you wish to feed. When they re-grow, chop them again. If you want to get even fancier, you can plant fast-growing species on purpose just so you can chop them down as mulch or compost. When various "weed" trees like mimosas or Florida holly or even poincianas show up in my food forest project, I don't chop them down to the ground. Instead, I trim around them and let them grow until they are over 6' tall, then chop them back to 6'. You can do this again and again and again, never letting the tree go to seed and using all its growth to feed other plants. Give the tree a few months to grow new branches and feed itself, then chop it back. All that growth can feed other things. In my gardens, I often pull weeds and throw them in the paths to dry out a bit so they don't re-root. When they are dead, I use them as mulch around my plants and in tire gardens. Chopping and dropping doesn't kill most weeds—it just keeps them down. I don't recommend letting a bunch of weeds grow in the middle of your vegetable garden. I also don't recommend cutting seedy weeds and mulching your veggies with them. It's a practice that works best in perennial systems, though I plan to experiment with deliberately planting some bunch grasses around the edges of my garden for quick, non-seedy mulching fodder.

Deep Mulching

Deep mulching was covered above. If you put down some cardboard, newspaper, palm fronds, or banana leaves, then stack mulch over that, you can effectively get rid of weeds. It rots fast, though, and you'll have to keep topping off your mulch to keep weeds from gaining a foothold. In small gardens, deep mulching can be a good option to keep the soil nice and keep weeds down. In a large survival garden, it's not the best option. You just have to work too hard to gain materials and keep dumping them. Better to hoe.

Flaming

Flame weeders work quite well for knocking down weeds in paths and in new garden areas. They're also tons of fun. They rely on propane, however, so if the entire world collapses you won't be able to run one. They aren't as good inside established gardens because it's too easy to torch your plants—and they're also dangerous in dry areas. The edges of pine woods are particularly dangerous areas to flame weed, as are pastures during a drought.

Herbicides

I used to have an uncle who would spray a large area of ground with RoundUp, wait a week or so, then dump a load of manure on the dead area, till it in, then plant his gardens. It worked well for him, though that was before we knew about the health dangers of glyphosate or the herbicide residues in cow manure. It was a simpler time. I do not recommend using herbicides to establish a garden. It's better to avoid toxins. The one exception I would make is if you're dealing with cogongrass. Cogongrass is the worst invasive species I have ever encountered. Back when I lived in North Florida, I fought it by hand, then finally gave in and killed it all with RoundUp. Even then, I had to spray more than once. The stuff creates underground stolons that run everywhere and pop up. I actually had them stick right through the center of a sweet potato and keep growing. It's a nasty, nasty grass that is almost impossible to eradicate through organic means. It came back in patches towards the back of my property for years even after I killed it in my nursery and garden area. After I moved from that property, the woman that bought it had family issues to take care of and was not able to stay on top of fighting the cogongrass. Last time I saw the backyard, it had become a sea of ugly grass around struggling mulberry and citrus and peach trees. Don't mess around with this stuff. KILL IT! I can't tell you how painful it was for me to give in to using herbicides, though. I really do not like them and have not used them since.

Hoeing

Hoeing is my favorite way to remove weeds. In the garden, we use a scuffle hoe or a common hoe for most tasks, knocking down young weeds weekly and keeping them from getting larger and going to seed. The paths are hoed with a Planet Whizbang Wheel Hoe as needed. When we clear new land for a garden, we use machetes to chop through woody perennials and then use a broad-bladed grape hoe from Easy Digging to scrape all the remaining weeds away. Its strong and broad blade works on tough weeds better than any other hoe I've tried. In Florida sand, it's almost as fast as sweeping a floor.

Solarization

The Florida sun is powerful and can be harnessed to kill weeds, especially during the summer. If you have a new area you want to garden or an old, weedy spring bed that you're not going to use again for some months, mow it, then cover the ground in plastic and let the sun bake the weeds for you. I use Dewitt Sunbelt woven landscape fabric for this, as it lets water in from above while denying sunlight to the ground beneath, plus it's a lot tougher than regular plastic sheeting. (No, they didn't pay me to mention them. I discovered the stuff thanks to Dave Taylor at Taylor Garden Nursery in Sparr, Florida and used it in my own nursery and gardens and was quite impressed. Maybe I should see if they'll sponsor my YouTube channel. Dewitt The Good! On second thought, maybe not.) After a few months of sun, you can remove the plastic and garden on the sand and remains of dead weeds beneath. They'll compost right into the ground. As an additional benefit, solarization reduces nematode populations.

Living With Weeds

Some weeds bother me more than others. I won't tolerate a single blade of cogongrass or spiny pigweed in my yard, but I'll let purslane, non-spiny amaranth, and chickweed wander through my gardens unless they're really in the way. Outside my gardens, I let banks of weeds grow on purpose. They are good hiding places for predatory species that feed on garden pests and many of them also attract bees, butterflies and other pollinators. Having some weeds growing in a mess just outside your garden can reduce your pest problems—we'll talk more on that in the next chapter.

Finally, for a lot more information on weeds and how to control them, I recommend my friend John Moody's book *Winning the War on Weeds*.

Chapter 8

PESTS

Pest Control

When you've invested hours of effort and bundles of love into your garden, nothing makes you angrier than big holes in a fruit or worms in your corn. Except maybe cutworms cutting seedlings off at the ground. Those really, really tick me off. The first response is to go total COMPOST YOUR ENEMIES mode and look for the nastiest chemical spray you can find.

Then you remember that you're going to have to eat the stuff you spray, so you start looking for alternatives. Maybe the bugs will hate being sprayed with garlic? Maybe if I blast them right between their beady little compound eyes with pepper spray? Maybe I can kill them all with something labeled "organic" and they'll die just as surely as if I busted out the DDT?

Maybe, but think of all those poor, poor springs that will go utterly silent! My approach is not always totally organic, but I also don't want to kill everything in my garden or add unnecessary toxins to my food. In this chapter I'll cover some pest control ideas that will help you get your plants through most of the worst attacks.

Nutrition and Avoiding Stress

Lynn Gillespie, Colorado farmer and author, shared with me her secret to growing healthy, pest-resistant plants. The key, she says, is in the soil. I have noticed this as well, as plants that grow fast and strong and with good nutrition usually shrug off insect and disease attacks, whereas weak, spindly, chlorotic, and ill plants seem to attract unwanted pests like a hot dame in a trucker bar. Unfortunately, it's hard to improve Florida sand, and the heat and humidity put a lot of stress on our crops. Planting in the proper season and feeding and watering beds and plants as best as you can will stave off some of the worst insect attacks.

Here's a case in point. Two of my sons planted watermelons this spring. One of them started his from seeds in a slightly shady area with rich, deep soil. The other planted his from transplants in a hot, rocky area. Transplants are already stressed by being taken from a kindly nursery environment and put in full sun and wind and soil that isn't as rich and spongy as that to which they are accustomed. They wilted and struggled, but my son was diligent in watering and weeding them. However, while they were struggling, they were attacked by beetles that chewed the leaves vigorously and managed to kill a few of the transplants no matter how my son tried to fight them.

Due to his regular attention, they pulled through that as well, only to start losing melons to blossom end rot as they fought with the hot, dry, rocky conditions. Meanwhile, my other son's bed of melons grew much faster from seeds than the transplants had done, running everywhere and producing a half-dozen decent melons. A few succumbed to rot and a few were chewed by beetles, but for the most part, the watermelons did well despite the travails of a tropical climate in the midst of a dry season. Both of my sons learned from the experience and are planting again.

Stressed plants do not do as well with pests. It's almost as if God designed insects to hunt down and kill unhealthy plants, cleaning them up so better-adapted plants can take their place. Insects are somehow drawn to ill plants and kick them over the edge. It's similar to how doctors will say that a person was killed by a specific disease, but it was because of "co-morbidities". Take good care of your plants and soil from the beginning and many pest problems cease to be big issues. Sure, there are times when a healthy plant gets destroyed (I caught a hornworm gnawing on a beautiful green tomato plant today), but it's less often than the sick ones get knocked out. Strive for well-fed, well-watered plants first before you blame all garden problems on pests. Remember that our garden vegetables are weaker than their wild kin and much tastier. Get them strong and happy and they will do better under attack.

Observation

The second line of defense against pest invasions is to spend time in your garden, paying attention to what is happening with your plants. If you put your garden in a far corner of your lot, you are less likely to visit it and see pest issues before they turn serious. Spend at least a little bit of every day walking the rows, picking produce, watering, and watching for pests. A hornworm caught when he is small can be removed, but if you catch him after he's eaten away the entire top of a plant, you're too late. Insects can be crushed in the garden, or you can bring a small bowl of water with a couple of drops of dish detergent in it and use it for summary executions via drowning. Insects do not always drown easily in water because they do not have lungs. They breathe through spiracles, which are tubes that transport air through their exoskeletons. If you add a little soap to the water, it breaks the surface tension that allows air bubbles to stay inside these spiracles, quickly drowning them.

If you see silver trails around chewed plants, you are dealing with snails or slugs. If you see shiny eggs on leaves, you might have some beetles coming soon… or caterpillars. It's easy to pick them off if you notice eggs before they hatch. Afterwards, they turn into nasty things that are harder to find. Many issues can be headed off before they are a big deal.

Control Through Creating Habitat

I mention in the portion on weed control that I like to leave some weeds around near the edges of my gardens. Beyond that, I also grow beds inside my gardens that are filled with perennials, both fruiting and blooming. One bed I planted contained a pomegranate and a persimmon tree, both of which can be kept at smaller sizes. Around their bases grew a perennial marigold, tea roses, Mysore raspberries, purple oxalis, a couple *Talinum* species, chives, oregano, a chayote that climbed over the pomegranate, American groundnut vines, and various other herbs and blooms. It was a thick, rambling mess of edible and beautiful plants that provided a perfect place for predators to live as well as a sanctuary for pollinators. The bed was permanent and well-mulched. Lizards and toads lived there, bees visited daily and butterflies flitted around it. Long ago, many farms had hedgerows that served a similar purpose. In those thick perennial oases a wide range of species could exist, keeping pests in check. Nature tends to balance itself if you give it a chance.

Intercropping

If you don't mind a little anarchy in your garden, consider planting different vegetables together in beds. Instead of a hundred feet of cabbages, you might plant a few cabbages, then a few basil, a few marigolds, a few beans, some corn, then more cabbages on down a row. It makes it harder for pests to move right down a row because you've broken up their buffet. Insects are often designed just to attack certain species and are unable to eat others. If you put a tomato hornworm on a corn plant, it will starve.

A variety of crops in a close space also emits different aromas that can keep flying insects from zeroing in on their favorite food to lay their eggs. One year I started a garden by tilling up a large area and throwing out a big range of seeds early in the later winter. I had turnips and canola, collards, lentils, chickpeas, and winter wheat. If you scatter seeds then toss sprinkle dry grass around to keep the ground moist and water it all well, you'll have a big green mess in no time. After this grew for a while, I started thinning around turnips and collards, chopping bits of the rest as mulch. As the weather warmed, I started pulling turnips and cutting new areas of the thick, green carpet and planting in pepper and other warm-season transplants. We had zero pest issues, plus we got plenty of food with little work. It's quite a messy way to garden, and my wife hated it because it confused her as much as it did the pests—but it worked!

Crop Rotation

Keep pest issues from building up by moving your crops around the garden from year to year. Some pests will live over the year in the soil or mulch around your plants. They expect to find the same species of plants growing above them the next year. If they wake up and find there's nothing above them that they like to eat, they die out. If you have a bad problem with a pest one year in a certain spot, don't plant the same thing there again the next year. Okra attracts nematodes like crazy. The first year they might do okay, but plant them again in the same soil and you often get shrunken, sickly okra plants that are too infested to produce a crop.

Pesticides

Pesticides should be the last thing you reach for when you have problems. If you've built a healthy ecosystem around your gardens and have fed and watered the plants well, it's often unnecessary to spray anything. Unfortunately, in tough times we don't always have the luxury of enough compost and good perennial beds and improved soil so we're stuck playing Angel of Death. It's okay. I won't judge you if you need to spray to grow food. It can take time to grow a garden ecosystem up to the point where it's healthy enough to grow everything you want. But I do not want you to use pesticides as a crutch.

Healthy plants in a polyculture just don't need to be sprayed, most of the time. Especially if you pick varieties of plants that are suited to Florida's climate. I had no pest issues with longevity spinach, yams, ivy gourd, cassava, collards, mulberries, chaya, or many other well-adapted crops. On the other hand, I had bad issues with white potatoes, cucumbers, summer squash, Hubbard squash, sweet corn, tomatoes, and Brussels sprouts. They are just tough to acclimate to Florida. If I want to grow them, I may have to resort to at least a little neem or, Gaia have mercy, Sevin dust to help them limp along.

When I was a kid I had aphid issues in my garden. They were absolutely covering my lettuces, so I decided to take a can of Raid from my parents' pantry and destroy them. It worked SUPER FAST, but it also killed all my lettuces. And thinking about it later, I shouldn't have eaten those lettuces after spraying them anyhow. Ah, the mind of a child...

In my gardens I have experimented with hot pepper sprays and garlic sprays. Florida pests seem to appreciate the extra seasoning on their vegetables and mostly shrug it off. Neem oil works better and is a natural product. Sevin works even better, but smells bad and is not natural. It can knock out ants and aphids, as well as protecting against vine borers at the base of squash vines. Malathion kills everything and smells like cat spray—I won't use it. Anything nastier than Sevin I won't use, and in Florida, I didn't even use that because I stuck to plants that thrived in the climate and weren't much bothered by insects.

If you're working with hot, dry, scrubland soil and have little organic matter and started your garden in a lawn without a good range of insect predators, you may have to use some pesticides. Build up your ecosystem over time, learn to feed and water well, and plant the easy crops in this book and you shouldn't have much trouble.

Solarizing

I wrote about solarization in my chapter on weeds, but it's also a good choice for reducing the nematode population in a troublesome bed. If you pull up a plant and see twisted and knotted roots, you have nematodes. Sometimes they're so bad they keep vegetables from producing. One of the answers is to roast the bed by putting plastic over it and letting the sun bake the soil beneath for a few months. Clear plastic is probably best, but black plastic works as well. This treatment will also kill off grubs and other pests in the soil. Your earthworm allies should be able to burrow deeper and escape the heat even as it bakes your smaller and less-mobile enemies.

Selected Pests and How to Defeat Them

Ants

Most ants aren't much trouble, with the exception of fire ants and certain black ants that deliver aphids to plants and tend them. We'll cover fire ants below, as they are in a class of their own. Ants you might encounter in the garden include carpenter ants and the common pyramid ant. Pyramid ants are a solid, light orange color and build hills with a single entrance in the top, like a pyramid without its cap. They move very quickly and do not bite. Leave them alone—they don't hurt anything, and they help hunt insects and loosen soil. I like to watch them and will occasionally toss garden pests onto their hills to be devoured. Some small black ants in Florida like to get into fruit trees and plants and spread aphids and scale insects, particularly the puffy white ones. If you have a lot of black mold on your citrus trees, it's often the result of this activity. The ants tend the scale insects which then leave droppings all over the tree, breeding mold. One way to stop this is to smear a ring of Vaseline around the base of the tree so the ants can no longer pass, then spray the tree with an insecticidal oil or neem—or both at the same time, as I did with my ailing grapefruit trees. Readers have also recommended a product to me called "Tanglefoot", which is supposed to be better than Vaseline as an ant barrier. I have not tried it myself.

Aphids

Keep a range of weeds and/or perennial beds growing near your garden as a hiding and breeding place for beneficial ladybugs. Do not spray aphids with pesticide at the first sign of infestation. A few are not a big deal. Just wash them off with the hose and watch for ants. If there are ants tending them, kill the hills if you can find them. Larger infestations of aphids generally occur on sick or stressed plants.

Sometimes I let them eat a few, as having some aphids around starts to attract ladybugs. If I really need to protect a crop—such as rare varieties I am saving seeds from or a crop I need for survival—and aphids swarm it, I will first spray them off with the hose. If that doesn't work, I will either use a liquid solution of Sevin or hit them with homemade nicotine insecticide.

Here's the recipe, as first shared in *Grow or Die: The Good Guide to Survival Gardening*:

Materials:

- *A generous handful of cigar butts*
- *An old pot*
- *Dish soap*
- *Spray bottle*
- *Coffee filter*

First, take your old pot, throw in the cigar butts, and cover them with a quart or so of water. If you don't have cigar butts available (you poor nonsmoker you—you're missing out), just buy a packet of rolling tobacco and use that. Chewing tobacco or pipe tobacco would likely work as well, though who knows what other weird stuff might be in chewing tobacco. Probably dead bugs and fiberglass. Now set your pot to boiling. This will make your whole house smell like a wet ashtray. Some people may like this, though my wife doesn't for some reason. I like to cook the tobacco for an hour or so and let all the nicotine seep out. Then I let it sit overnight to steep even more. After it's turned into scary black tobacco water, pour it through a coffee filter into a spray bottle (this requires a funnel), and add a few drops of dish soap. Congratulations! You've made a viciously toxic insecticide! Don't leave it out where your kids can drink it or CIA agents can steal it for assassination attempts on unlikable dictators. I made a couple of batches of this and went around spraying things to see what would happen. One group of aphids I sprayed on one of my grapevines as a test initially looked fine. When I came back the next day, they were still there... but they were dead. And blackened.

Like a lung.

Bahfeemus

If you find round, olive-green eggs about the size of a bowling ball in your garden, do not touch them. Run away—do not walk—and never return to your property. It's not worth the risk. They are the eggs of a bahfeemus.

The bahfeemus is a massive reptilian creature with a terrifying gaping mouth filled with teeth. Its skin has the appearance of rubbery pink plastic. A bahfeemus cannot be killed and if you encounter one, you will die. If a bahfeemus appear in your dreams and you feel a sudden urge to bite your neighbor's goats, DO NOT FOLLOW YOUR DREAMS. Flee the area immediately.

Cabbage Moths

Cabbage moth larva will chew holes in the leaves of cabbages and sometimes get into the heads. Usually the damage is limited to the outer few leaves. We pick them off as we see them, but they aren't a problem every year. If you have caterpillars, Bt (*Bacillus thuringiensis*) is a good way to knock them out if you feel like you need to spray something. I've not used it. Instead, I've found the best way to avoid cabbage moths and other cabbage pests is to grow cabbage early in the season. The later it gets in the year, the more things attack cabbages.

Corn Ear-Worms

Corn ear worms are the larva of a moth that lays its eggs at the end of developing ears of corn. When you harvest the ears, you'll find a fat caterpillar in there and multiple destroyed kernels of corn. Some varieties of corn resist the moth better, due to their tight husks.

Some people put some mineral oil in the silk of corn a week after pollination, but I don't bother. Usually we only lose a few kernels, and I have too much corn to hand-treat every ear. Knock the worm out by some bushes so the lizards will eat him and save the rest of the corn.

Cutworms

Cutworms are my most-hated garden pest. They are monsters, appearing in the night to cut down young seedings and transplants. They take a bite through the stem and leave the top of the plant laying on the ground. Once your plants get a little bigger these worms are no longer an issue, but early

Avoid encountering a bahfeemus at all costs.

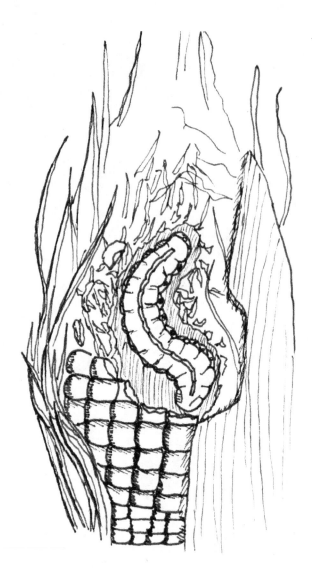

The corn ear-worm happily chews through the top kernels on an ear of corn.
(Drawing by my eldest son)

on they can be devastating. Cutworms hide in organic matter and mulch, so if you deep mulch (which I do not in my main beds), they may be more of an issue.

This year I experimented with putting a ring of ashes around each seedling in the garden. It seemed to help some but was not infallible. The best way to beat cutworms is to put a hard ring of something around each seedling. We have used paper-towel and toilet paper rolls cut into 2" tall rings. We've also used tin cans or soda cans with the top and bottom cut off. Rings cut from plastic water bottles work as well and, like tin cans, are reusable. Press your cutworm protectors into the ground a little so the marauding nasties won't get underneath.

Seriously, I hate these things. If you're going to attack something in my garden, don't just take one bite and kill it. It's a total waste! They will knock a plant down with one bite through the stem and leave the entire top laying on the ground untouched, then go on and cut another seedling down. It's like squirrels eating one bite from a fruit and dropping it, then taking another fruit and doing the same thing—but more on tree rats in a minute.

Deer

Deer are a devastating marauder. If you live in deer country, the best defense is an 8' fence around your gardens. The second best defense is some good dogs that will chase them away from your gardens. My friend Marjory Wildcraft has said her dogs are the only thing that truly keeps her gardens safe from deer. Of course, if you can't manage to keep the deer out of your garden, you can eat them. Venison > lettuces.

Fire Ants

An old Florida redneck trick for killing fire ants is to pour a little gasoline into the top of a hill and let it soak in for a minute, then tossing a match on it. Florida Man says "You like fire, FIRE ANTS? I'LL GIVE YOU FIRE!" The resultant string of burning and smoke that appears in a whoosh of flame that sometimes emerges from tunnels feet away is quite satisfying, but I would never, ever, ever recommend doing this. No, no matter how fun it is. No matter how much you hate them.

I, of course, am too virtuous to even consider such a method and already feel bad that I wrote it down here. A safer method to kill them without poisons is to boil a pot of water and pour it right down through the center of a hill, steaming thousands of teeming ants and their maggoty little babies, hopefully along with their vile queens. This is not a good method inside garden beds because you will also hurt plant roots and foliage close to the pile. I have used Amdro™ ant bait for fire ants and it works well. It's also less toxic than most pesticide alternatives. Another option is to dust a little Sevin over piles, which usually wipes them out in a day.

Hornworms

The best way to deal with hornworms is to watch your tomatoes and tobacco religiously. Seriously. Go out there and pray against the worms! They are evil!

Actually, you really just need to keep your eyes on your tomatoes and tobacco. A friend once told me he'd been away from his garden for a few days and came back to find all his lush tomato plants had been turned into leafless stems by ravenous hornworms. Hornworms are big, fat caterpillars with voracious appetites. They are the exact same green as the plant they're eating which sometimes makes them hard to spot.

If you see an area that has been stripped of leaves—usually at the top of a plant—start hunting. The hornworm is around somewhere. When you find him, throw him in your DFSW barrel to rot down as plant fertilizer or, more amusingly, feed him to an ant pile. Other disposal methods include drowning, burning alive, firing from a slingshot, or frying in a pan to serve as a tiny entree. Tomato hornworms taste rather like french fries. Tobacco hornworms I don't dare ingest, but it's possible they could be dried and

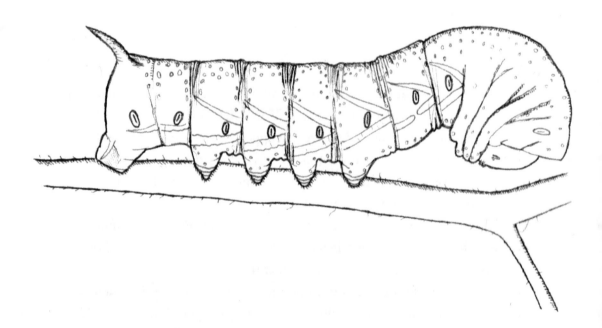

This illustration by my eldest son depicts a hornworm in all his majestic creepiness.
(Drawing by my eldest son)

smoked.

Hornworms are the caterpillar form of various types of sphinx moths, which I find quite beautiful, so long as they stay out of my garden. A cousin of tomato and tobacco hornworms is the bright, striped caterpillar that periodically defoliates Florida's frangipani trees.

If you can catch hornworm eggs in your garden before they hatch, that is even better. Look on the bottom of leaves for little green eggs. They make poor omelets, so just crush them. *The Farmer's Almanac* recommends planting dill, basil, and marigolds between your tomatoes as a repellent, which may keep adult moths confused enough to skip your garden. If not, at least you have herbs and pretty flowers to comfort you over the loss of your tomatoes. Then again, you're not likely to get good tomatoes in Florida, hornworms, or no hornworms.

A final note on hornworms: if you find one with white, fluffy eggs on his back, let him live. He has been parasitized by a wasp and will soon succumb to the grubs burrowing into his guts. These will later turn into wasps that will happily keep hunting hornworms for you.

Leaf Miners

Leaf miners are a tiny insect that lives in between the tissues in plant leaves, leaving distinctive winding trails on the leaf's surface as they feed and grow. Because they live inside the leaves, spraying is ineffective. They can do quite a bit of damage to citrus leaves, causing the infected leaves to twist and curl, but the damage is never too much for the tree to handle. If you see their trails on the leaves in your gardens, you can ignore them or pluck off and destroy infected leaves. Once you notice the damage, it's often too late, and the bug is already gone. We just ignore them.

Leaf-Footed Bugs

Leaf-footed bugs punch holes in tomatoes and peppers, sometimes causing the fruits to rot from secondary bacterial or fungal infections. Drown them in soapy water, knocking them in as best as you can. You could probably spray as well, but I have not bothered.

Usually, they appear later in the season when most of my crops are already in. Observing early planting times is a big help in avoiding the worst plague insects.

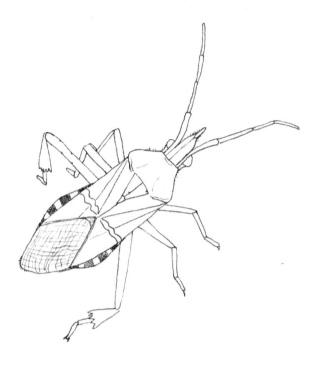

The leaf-footed bug is a common invader of Florida gardens during the summer months.
(Drawing by my eldest son)

Nematodes

Root-knot nematodes are a big problem in Florida sand. They are microscopic worms that burrow into plant roots and make big lumps out of them, reducing the host's ability to take up water and nutrients, stunting its growth, and sometimes leading to its early demise. I've had nematode damage show up on okra, beans, tomatoes, and even pak choi roots. Peaches are very susceptible to nematode damage in Florida, which is why nursery trees are grafted onto nematode-resistant rootstock. That said, I grew many seedling peaches in Florida sand and had luck keeping them going thanks to lots of organic matter and mulch. Nematodes do not thrive in compost-rich soil. They also don't thrive if you keep the ground clear of plant life. That's right—if you turn your backyard into a tiny Sahara, the nematodes will eventually starve and go away. Since this is neither advisable nor practical, I practice crop rotation, add compost to beds, and sometimes solarize areas to knock back bad infestations. There are reports that tilling cabbage leaves into the soil will greatly reduce populations, but I have not tried it. Mustard is also supposed to repel nematodes. I have grown it as a cover crop and chopped bunches of it to throw around my peach trees. Fertilizing with neem cake is also supposed to repel nematodes, but I've never seen it anywhere. So far as I know there is no sure-fire way to get rid of nematodes in the garden but healthy soil and higher organic matter levels will mitigate the damage, as will keeping plants happy with feeding and watering.

Scale Insects

Kill ants if they are accompanying the scale insects. Crush small infestations with your fingers. Try spraying nicotine insecticide or neem. Generally these have not been an issue in my garden, though I have had outbreaks on fruit trees.

Squirrels

Squirrels can be shot with a .22 or a pellet gun to reduce populations. I have also taken them out with a "wrist rocket" slingshot. I used to have a neighbor when I lived in Tennessee who would trap all the squirrels in the neighborhood so they wouldn't bother his gardens. It led to a huge reduction in population over a couple of years. I highly recommend having lots of children and training them in marksmanship. Squirrels are edible but not great. Fallen squirrels can be buried in Melon Pits or under corn stations, or thrown into the middle of your compost pile. If you're really hardcore, they can also be chopped into pieces and fed to chickens as a source of protein. If you are a tender soul, you can put netting over fruit trees to keep ripening fruit safe from squirrels, though some trees are way too large for this treatment. Shoot them. You know you want to. PEW PEW PEW PEW PEW!

Stink Bugs

Treat as you would leaf-footed bugs.

Vine Borers

These are the pests that kill my summer squash and my beloved Blue Hubbards, regularly ruining our hopes for more northerly squash varieties. The vine borer is a nasty little insect that lays its eggs near the base of your pumpkin or squash vines. An egg hatches, and the resultant grub goes chewing his happy way through the inside of the vine where you can't see him. Wilting leaves reveal the invader—and by then, it's usually too late. If you're a good bug hunter, you can sometimes look for the damaged portion on the vine and use a needle or razor to destroy the grub. Usually it's no use, though, as your plant is already at death's door.

There are a few ways to fight back. The first is cultural. As your pumpkin vines grow, they will root from below their leaf nodes. I deliberately mound little hills of soil over leaf nodes and keep weeds away so the vines are encouraged to make even more roots into the ground. If there are plenty of rooted areas on a pumpkin vine, it matters less if borers take one piece of it. This is also why I do not recommend growing pumpkins on trellises or fences. On the ground, they root repeatedly. They don't do this when they are suspended in the air and therefore are much more likely to be destroyed by a borer.

I once found a very sweet pumpkin at a roadside stand and saved seeds. It was the only one I'd ever seen of that kind and I was excited to grow it. I cleared an area at the edge of some brush and made a hill, then planted seeds. They grew and ran in all directions, but the best of all the vines headed up into the brush, climbing lithely over a small tree and up into the air. Meanwhile, the weather got worse, and the other vines gave up, leaving me only this one in the tree. To my delight, it bloomed and started to make a pumpkin just like its parent. Then disaster struck. While the pumpkin was still very under-ripe, vine borers attacked the base of the vine. One day I passed and saw the pumpkin growing and the vine healthy, the next I came back to find the entire vine wilting. The result was that the pumpkin never matured and I lost the variety. If it had been running on the ground, it might have withstood the attack. With only one rooting point it didn't stand a chance.

This is why bushy summer squash and the-loathsome-vegetable-that-shall-not-be-named-though-it-starts-with-Z can be hard to grow in Florida. They do not have long, rambling vines that can root repeatedly, so one hit from a borer and BAM—they are dead.

A second way to deal with vine borers is to spray repeatedly. Neem reportedly keeps them away when sprayed regularly, as does a dusting of Sevin around the base of vines, though if you grow Seminole pumpkins and other varieties adapted well to Florida and encourage them to root at all the nodes, it's not necessary to spray anything.

Disease Control

As with pests, the best approach to disease control is to grow healthy plants by feeding and watering well.

Powdery mildew

Powdery mildew shows up as a white, dusty-looking coating on some plant leaves. It's common on pumpkins and squash and sometimes on beans. Generally, I find it to be a disease of already declining plants and I don't bother treating it. If you plant early in the year and don't soak your plants too much, especially with overhead watering at night, it's not usually a problem. I have treated it successfully by putting a few tablespoons of yogurt into a quart of rain or well water (no chlorine!) and misting plant leaves with it.

Wilt diseases

Sometimes a plant looks very happy and healthy, then the next day it wilts, then yellows, then browns, no matter how much you water it. This has been a big problem for me with growing tomatoes in tropical climates. It has also killed sunflowers, pomegranates and beans. They look good, and then they don't. I do not have a sure-fire cure for this issue, but if it happens to you, it's a good idea to avoid planting similar plants in the same space the next season. It's also good to avoid overhead watering in the evening.

To wrap this chapter up, remember that taking good care of your plants and keeping them well-fed and watered is the first line of defense against pests and diseases. Healthy, happy, satisfied plants will shrug off most issues. Spray and pick and dust as you must, just make sure you take care of plant and soil health first.

Chapter 9

LONG-TERM FLORIDA SURVIVAL GARDENING

My approach to gardening in Florida has proven remarkably successful. I started by experimenting, growing everything I was interested in, starting with vegetable gardening as a child then later planting trees and shrubs and seeds and garden beds wherever I wanted and seeing what happened. I traded for seeds, bought exotic plants, pushed my growing zone, composting everything I could, watched permaculture videos, read tons of books, planted a big variety of different things every year, dug beds, planted right in the sand, tried Mel Bartholomew's Square Foot Gardening, tried John Jeavons' Biointensive gardening, tried Steve Solomon's methods in *Gardening When It Counts* (which I prefer over the other two methods), planted multiple food forests, grafted fruit trees, learned the names of most of the wild plants, tried my hand at growing mushrooms, raised ducks, goats, rabbits, chickens, and guinea fowl, did vermicomposting, launched a plant nursery, experimented with different compost pile types... it's been a long, long string of experiments, all of which taught me a little more every year about what works in the state of Florida. Once you reach an expert level of gardening prowess, you will no longer fear failure. They roll over you and you learn from them. If you follow the advice in this book, you won't have to spend decades experimenting and failing and succeeding then failing again. There's no time for that now—this is a book on survival gardening! We need to have success, not just now but in future years.

Annual gardens will feed you this year. Perennials will feed you for years to come.

The great thing about gardening is that it gets easier and easier to harvest big yields as you improve your land and plant long-term perennial crops.

The first year you plant berries, you might get a handful. It gets better in the second and third year as you keep mulching and feeding and watering, and the plants mature and hit their stride. A little skinny peach tree with a single bloom one year can turn into a monster, producing buckets of peaches in its third or fourth year. This is why you should plant at least a few shrubs and trees every year along with your annual gardens. As they come into production, they take less work to maintain and produce tons of food without you having to dig and till and water. The citrus trees I planted back in 2012–13 are now making hundreds of pounds of fruit. The mulberries are making buckets and buckets of berries. The loquats are countless. The yam bulbils I planted have grown into huge roots that take care of themselves, dying back and regenerating every year until they are dug and eaten. The bananas are bearing bunches and bunches.

With annual gardens you start anew every year, toiling and planting and digging and weeding. With perennials, the yields increase year after year to insane levels with just a little care. Florida has a climate that is wonderful for fruit. In fact, it's better suited to growing trees and shrubs than growing annual gardens. From Central on down through South Florida you can grow quite a few tropical species that take a little cold, like starfruit and guavas. From Central Florida north, you can grow many temperate species like peaches, pears and apples, blueberries and blackberries, plus some mild-climate fruits like figs and pomegranates. In sunny South Florida, most of the tropics are open to you, allowing you to grow ackee and mangoes and lychee and jackfruit. It's a paradise for rare fruit growers, though the freer and less-populated counties farther north are a better place to ride out tough times.

In this chapter, we'll take a look at how you can feed yourself both today and years from now. When I was growing up there was a giant grapefruit tree in my parents' backyard. It produced hundreds of pounds of grapefruit yearly, despite not being watered or fertilized or pruned or sprayed. It over-supplied us with wagonloads of sweet white grapefruit for decades before it finally died of old age and disease. Now in its place is a mini food forest filled with smaller trees my parents and I planted a decade ago. Mom was given a mango tree by the city, and it is now a heavy producer of perfect fruit. I planted a starfruit and two mulberries, which are loaded with berries multiple times per year. Off to the side of the yard is a chocolate pudding fruit tree that bears buckets of exotic and delicious fruit. There's a coconut palm filled with nuts. A small Key Lime that bears faithfully. A few Surinam cherry bushes bearing their sweet-tart aromatic cherries. Moringa trees, covered in edible leaves and pods. Katuk and chaya; excellent no-care greens. A large tamarind tree shades the driveway, loaded with sweet pods. And there are yams making vines through the middle of everything, leaving fat roots behind to be dug when wanted. Mind you, this is a yard with that "awful sugar sand" in it. Annual gardens are a chore to maintain in that soil, but a long-term perennial system has been thriving there and bearing for years. The first few years establishing it were tough going. Some of the trees died. Others just sat and did nothing. There never seemed to be enough rain, or time, or whatever, to make things grow as well as we wanted. I did not live nearby so the food forest was sometimes overlooked... but it held on, pushed through, and as hundreds of visitors can testify, it is now an oasis of greenery and fantastic fruit.

This isn't a book on food forests or orchards or vineyards. It's a book on survival gardening, which generally means the reader is at the "oh shoot, I should grow food now!" stage. I totally understand. As the pandemic loomed, I planted lots of corn, pumpkins, sweet potatoes, cassava, beans, and pigeon peas—not fruit trees! Your main focus should be on annuals right now, but don't focus on them alone. The gardens you are building right now will not last past this year without you rebuilding and replanting. All the hard work of raking and hoeing and digging and planting and watering and feeding and harvesting—gone! Walk away from an annual garden and you'll have nothing to show for your hard work in a few months. It'll all be eaten by sand and weeds. But if you plant fruit trees at the same time, you'll be growing a long-term strategic reserve of food that will make your life easier in years to come.

Let's run through some simple garden plans based on common Florida yards. I have secured the help of Todd Jordan, a very good landscape architect, to give you an idea of what can be done.

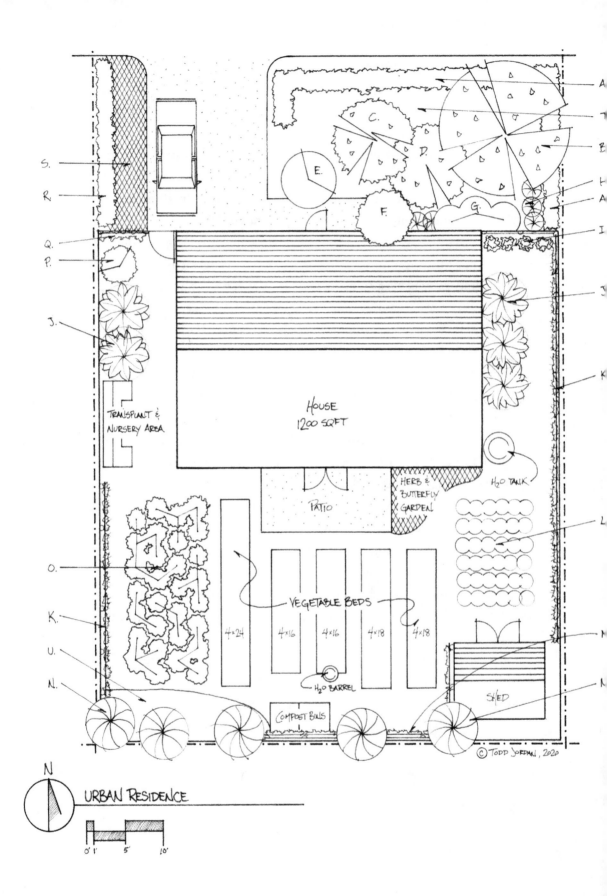

S.

R.

Q.

P.

J.

O.

K.

U.

N.

A.

T.

B.

H.

A.

I.

J.

K.

L.

N.

N.

C.

D.

E.

F.

G.

TRANSPLANT & NURSERY AREA

HOUSE 1200 SQFT

PATIO

HERB & BUTTERFLY GARDEN

H₂O TANK

VEGETABLE BEDS

4x24   4x16   4x16   4x18   4x18

H₂O BARREL

COMPOST BINS

SHED

© TODD JORDAN, 2020

N

URBAN RESIDENCE

0' 1'   5'   10'

A Survival Garden Plan for a Small South Florida Yard

This first plan is for a small suburban South Florida home on a 1/10 acre lot. Top is North. The lot is 70' x 90' with a 1,200 square foot home in the middle.

If the front yard is kept well-maintained, you can generally get away with whatever you like in your backyard, provided you have a fence. I highly recommend a privacy fence around the backyard if you can afford it. A wooden fence should cost less than $2,000 and will spare you from prying eyes and calls to code enforcement. It also makes your garden feel more like a private oasis from the madness of the world.

The trees in the front yard can be pruned to keep them small, or you can plant less and let them run up to full size. I recommend topping mango trees when small and letting them make multiple side trunks. Otherwise they will get gigantic and drop fruit from a mile up. The edges of tree canopies can overlap a little, but you shouldn't let large fruit trees completely overshadow smaller fruit trees, or the smaller tree will be unlikely to bear much—if any—fruit. A chaya hedge is quite serviceable, but if you'd like something prettier, cattley guavas, pineapple guava, cocoplum, or Surinam cherries will fill in nicely and produce edible fruit. If you mulch the front yard and plant sweet potato slips, you can get quite decent yields as they run around under the trees as a ground cover. It is surprisingly attractive as well. The key lime in

---

Plant Schedule

A. Edible Mixed Hedge

B. Mango Tree with Yams in Canopy

C. Acerola Cherry

D. Starfruit

E. Key Lime

F. Guava

G. Surinam Cherry

H. Pineapple

I. Perennial Cucumbers

J. Bananas in Greywater

K. Bean Trellises

L. Sweet Potatoes

M. Trellised Mixed Perennials

N. Coconut Palm

O. Cassava

P. Jaboticaba

Q. Passionfruit Trellis

R. Edible Chaya Hedge

S. Edible Landscaping

T. Sweet Potato Yard Groundcover

U. Seminole Pumpkins

front is a must-have in South Florida. It just is. A plastic flamingo at the base of it is optional, though.

On to the back yard. Cassava is a survival mainstay and is perfect for South Florida. The thirty plants in the illustration, if well-tended, should give you about 300 lbs of cassava in a year. If interplanted with bush beans, you'll get an additional five-gallon bucket or so of green beans or a gallon or two of dried beans along with it.

Your main vegetable garden beds can be used both for calorie and nutrition crops. In fall, winter and spring, beds can be pressed into service for cool-season staples like cabbage and turnips. Daikon radishes, collards, lettuce, kale, and mustard are other good choices. It's very easy to grow all the salad greens you desire by dedicating a single bed in fall to the production of a range of greens. Go to the seed rack and buy some salad green mixes, along with radishes, lettuces, spinaches, and whatever else looks good to you. Prepare a nice seed bed and sprinkle seeds all across it, then rake in the seeds and water. Soon you'll have a gigantic bed of salad greens and radishes.

Through the spring and summer your main beds can be cropped with black-eyed peas and okra, as well as sweet potatoes and grain corn. In South Florida, you can also grow most warm-season crops right through the winter, though the cool-season crops won't handle the summer heat. Be sure to plant even most of your warm season crops early in the year—January to February—or the heat, humidity, pounding rain, and pests of summer will reduce your yields. Note that I dedicated a big bed to sweet potatoes outside the main gardens. After cassava, sweet potatoes are a top survival crop that will help keep you full. The bed is 9' x 14', which can easily net you 150 lbs of sweet potatoes.

Your garden beds are only 368 square feet of gardening space. At least half of this can be devoted to calorie crops and you'll still have plenty of space for more nutrient-dense nutrition crops. You'll be surprised how many greens you can get from that amount of space.

Around the edges of the backyard are multiple trellises which will keep you absolutely loaded down with beans, cucumbers, passionfruit, malabar spinach, chayote squash, true yams, and whatever other climbers you care to grow on them. The vertical space along a fence can be fantastically productive and it's easy to run some strings or wire down the side of a wooden privacy fence. I also recommend a patch in a corner for the excellent

Seminole pumpkin. Hemming it in back there will help it from running over everything.

In the "mixed perennials" and "mixed hedge" area of this plan you can go crazy. Pineapple guavas, Simpson stoppers, mulberries, coffee, Mysore raspberries (which are truly tropical!), katuk, chaya, edible-leaf hibiscus, cattley guava, Surinam cherries, neem, kumquats, limeberry, clumping bamboo, monstera, gingers, pineapples, grenadilla, hot peppers, *Pereskia spp.*, cocoplum, sea grapes, moringa, and more. The possibilities for mixed hedges are incredible. Consider it a 2D food forest—and do not neglect pruning as needed.

Note that I also include a two-bin compost pile and a wider path leading to it from the house. Each bin is 4' x 4', which will handle all your garden waste along with kitchen scraps and hedge prunings. If you want faster compost, do not add hedge prunings. Instead, I recommend making another pile somewhere in the yard for the woodier stuff and letting it rot down over a year or two by itself. Near the compost is a moringa tree, which can be kept cropped for leaves and for "green" material for the compost pile.

A water tank off the roof is a very good idea. If you can get an 800-gallon tank from Tractor Supply, it will serve you quite well—and a good rain will fill it up! A roof gathers a lot more water than you might think. Rainwater is better than city water by a long shot as it does not contain chlorine and fluoride. Garden yields are higher when chlorine is absent.

Coconut palms can be considered a survival gardening staple in South Florida. The nuts are highly nutritious and filling when fully ripe and can be processed to make coconut oil and coconut milk. The coconut water in immature nuts is excellent for your health and can stand in for lunch when you're working in the garden. I find that it fills me up and reinvigorates me as I farm.

Bananas and plantains are reliable producers of fruit if they are watered and fed heavily, hence my placing them beside the house. If you can clandestinely run a washing machine drain out into a couple clumps of bananas on one side of the house and a shower or sink drain out into the bananas on the other side, they'll get all the water they need. The more grey water you can send outside into bananas, the better. It allows you to get two uses from the water and it will also grow you lots and lots of bananas. Getting 40–80 lbs of bananas from one stand of bananas per year is not hard.

This design should net you around 200–400 lbs per year if you can use grey water. If you want to grow even more bananas, you can intercrop them with sweet potatoes in the back yard or take out a garden bed for a few more clumps. Veggies can be grown around their bases to a limited extent. Seminole pumpkins are a good bet. However, if bananas are growing in the yard without grey water, you will have to give them lots of supplementary water. Bananas are lousy producers otherwise.

If you can also grow a jaboticaba, do it. They can produce as many as five crops a year. If you irrigate and mulch it, it will thrive and grow to maturity much faster than if you just let the rain water it.

Finally, Todd and I discussed adding orange trees to these plans, but I have decided not to include them due to how disease-prone citrus has become in Florida. Greening often takes out citrus trees, so you are unfortunately better off skipping them.

Annual yields

Here are some estimates on yields. This is quite a rough guess on my part, but is based on my own experiences. If you feed and care for your gardens and grow high-yield crops, you can beat it easily.

- Acerola cherry: 15 lb
- Bananas: 300 lb
- Cassava: 300 lb
- Coconuts: 500 lb
- Front-yard yams: 100 lb
- Guava: 30 lb
- Herbs: 10 lb
- Jaboticaba: 20 lb
- Mango: 150 lb
- Mixed hedges: 350 lb (could easily range from 100–500 lb, depending on species planted)
- Perennial cucumbers: 25 lb
- Pineapples: 20 lb
- Seminole pumpkin: 50lb
- Starfruit: 150 lb
- Sweet potato bed and front-yard sweet potatoes: 200 lb

- Various trellised crops: 200 lb
- Vegetable gardens: 500 lb
- Yams 75 lb

Total yield: 2,995 lbs

And this is on 1/10 acre! Aren't you glad you're in Florida? Tropical crops can be marvelously productive and we can grow year-round gardens. Plus we have the best beaches, though that has nothing to do with survival. Unless you count our need for Vitamin D.

This little yard plan is just to give you some ideas. It assumes a South Florida, USDA zone 10/11 climate that allows coconuts and mangoes and other tropical plants.

Let's move a little north and create a plan for a larger yard in USDA zone 8/9. Here's a half-acre homestead plan.

Plant Schedule

A. Yaupon Hedge
B. Figs
C. Pecan Tree with Yams in Canopy
D. Supply Staging Area
E. Blackberry Hedge
F. Bananas in Greywater
G. Nursery Area
H. 8x12 Transplant Greenhouse
I. Edible Perennial Hedge
J. True Yams on Trellises
K. Cassava
L. Sweet Potatoes
M. Trellised Mixed Perennials
N. Potatoes
O. Grain Corn
P. Seminole Pumpkins
Q. Grape Trellises
R. Perennial Cucumbers
S. Herbs and Perennials
T. Plum
U. Soapnut Tree Cluster
V. Mixed Perennial Hedge
W. Mulberry
X. Peach
Y. White Mulberry
Z. Pomegranate
AA. Loquat

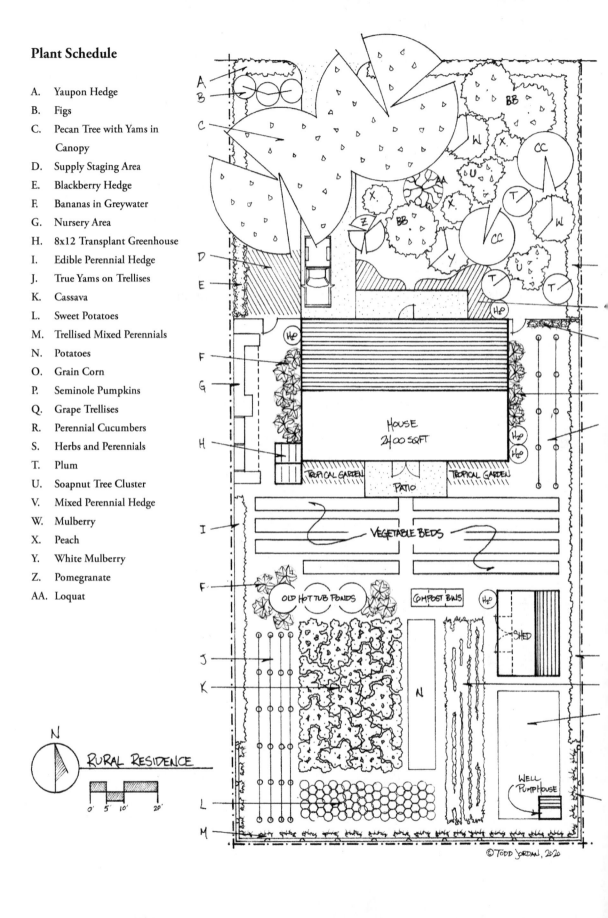

RURAL RESIDENCE

0'   5'   10'   20'

© TODD JORDAN, 2020

A Survival Garden Plan for a Larger North Florida Yard

If you go farther north in the state, you will not be able to grow some of the tropical plants that thrive in South Florida's almost frost-free climate. Coconuts disappear quickly, which is a painful loss. Then you lose Acerola cherries, then mangoes. You start to gain a few species, however, such as persimmons, blueberries, peaches, blackberries, apples, pears, pecans, and chestnuts. Cassava takes longer to grow and will freeze down in winter, but it is still a top survival crop.

In this half-acre plan, you'll note that the vegetable gardens are still outside the back door of the house, but beyond them we have a large area dedicated to less-demanding high-calorie field crops. The compost pile has been in-creased in size to a three-bin system with 4' x 4' bins in a row. Behind it are some moringa trees, which can be repeatedly cropped to add some "green" material to the compost pile, as well as for nutritious leaves for the table. Three old hot tubs are placed in the garden area for backup water/ponds, which should also be used to grow aquatic plants such as water hyacinth, azolla, and water lettuce in order to create extra nitrogen layers for the compost pile.

The larger house has enough roof to easily fill 4,000 gallons worth of water tanks in a couple of good, Florida rains, and the roof of the shed/workshop gets its own tank—perhaps a 600 gallon. Additionally, there is a well in the back yard. Between the hot tubs and the water tanks, you have a solid 5,500–6,000 gallons of water in reserve for irrigation and even drinking (after filtration) if need be. One side benefit of the tanks, though I don't show it here, is that tropical plants such as passionfruit can easily be grown next to them due to the thermal mass of water which prevents freezing on cold nights. Bananas are harder to grow in North Florida, but they are by no means impossible. They need plenty of water and feeding in the warm months to help them overcome the frosts of winter and still bloom.

Along the west side of the house is a larger nursery area and a small greenhouse that will allow you to keep tender species alive through winter as well as get a head-start on warm season crops by starting transplants. If you add six or eight sealed 55-gallon drums filled with water along the edges of the greenhouse, you will not need to heat it as they will moderate the temperatures inside, both keeping plants from freezing on cold nights and from baking on hot, sunny days. The drums can be stood up and used as the bases to planting benches, thus serving more than one function.

In the front yard you have a variety of temperate and sub-tropical species to choose from. The three easiest-to-grow North Florida fruit trees are the mulberry, the persimmon, and the loquat. All three are virtually care-free and do not take up a ton of space. Note that the white-fruited mulberry is near the house, and the regular black mulberries are out in the yard. White mulberry fruit don't make a purple mess so you can plant them closer. Peaches are more demanding but worth the work. Pomegranates sometimes thrive and sometimes die. Figs are easy, provided they have good drainage, full sun, and some organic matter in the soil.

Two big benefits of living farther north in the state are the addition of pecans and chestnuts as food sources. Both are excellent survival crops. Pecans take their sweet time to produce, but chestnuts only take a few years. You need at least two of each for pollination. Pears are usually easy to grow from Central Florida on north, but you need to plant a couple of those for pollination as well. My favorite is the old-fashioned "Pineapple" pear. Pair it with a Hood and a Baldwin or a Flordahome.

Generally I like to plant three of each type of fruit tree, especially when cross-pollination is required. This way if I lose one of two mature trees to a blight, I don't have to plant a new sapling and wait for it to start blooming to pollinate my remaining mature tree. Blackberries make decent hedges, especially the large improved types from the University of Arkansas. You'll see a blackberry hedge on the western border of the yard. Plant thorny selections to keep out invaders or thornless ones if you'd rather pick without getting torn up. I plant both. If you have pine woods in your area or pines in your yard, blueberries will likely be your best berry crop.

By the street on the west side of the drive, there is a small hedge of yaupon holly, which is a common landscape plant in Florida. The leaves can be made into a refreshing, caffeinated tea. Caffeine is very important during the apocalypse. On the other side of the drive is a blueberry hedge. If you do not have pines, amend the soil with lots of rotten pine bark dug in deeply around where you intend to plant. Mulch with pine bark or pine needles.

The eastern edge of the front yard is a mixed perennial hedge, which can also be used to line the edges of the back yard. I am a huge fan of these systems, if you hadn't noticed. You can grow a big mess of food and useful plants in a hedgerow. In North Florida, species might include cattley guava (which is more cold-hardy than tropical guava), feijoa, blackberries, Mysore raspberries, yaupon holly, chaya, Chickasaw plum, dwarf mulberries, blueberries, deerberry, sparkleberry, Simpson stoppers, kumquats, peaches, pyracantha, flowering almond (for bees), staghorn sumac, goumi berries, autumn olive, pomegranates, clumping bamboo, moringa, figs, and more. The sky is the limit. Plant a mess of edible and useful plants. Throw in some flowers if you like, like azaleas or cassias. Prune however you wish. If you have my book *Free Plants for Everyone*, you already know how to propagate thousands of dollars worth of plants in your backyard. It's a huge savings over buying plants! That's why I always include a little nursery area in whatever homestead I am building or planning.

In the front yard food forest system, try to avoid overcrowding of your fruit trees as that will actually decrease yields. Space a little wider, then you can also plant lots of sweet potatoes and various perennials such as ginger and arrowroot and berries beneath the trees, not to mention lots and lots of climbing yams. Alternatively, if you want more fruit and nut tree varieties, plant denser and prune heavily to keep the trees small.

Back to the back yard. As before, the vegetable gardens are just outside the back patio area where you'll see them and be able to head off problems before they occur. If you are a smoker—or if you want barter material—a portion of one of these beds can be dedicated to growing tobacco. Your main seasons in Central and North Florida are spring and fall. The "dead" time of year for gardening is in the heat of summer, as temperatures often soar into the 90s and 100s, which will keep you from growing much. I recommend sowing a summer cover crop of black-eyed peas to add organic matter and nitrogen or covering unused beds with plastic to roast insects and weeds until fall.

Muscadine grapes grow very well in Florida and are not hard to tend, provided a good wire is provided for climbing and grapes are pruned well in late winter. You will find my video on how to prune grapes online—it's simple. The area provided on the northeast corner of the back yard is enough space for a dozen vines (six in each 42' bed) which will bear gallons and gallons of grapes after three years in the ground.

There is one exciting thing about living in the northern half of the state which most gardeners have not tapped into and that is the amazing power of a south-facing wall. Along the southern wall of your house you can grow truly tropical crops right through winter. They may not grow much in the cold, but they will live through freezes. In North Florida I kept a key lime tree planted right against my wall, along with black pepper, various perennial tropical greens, kaffir lime, guavas, and even a small coffee tree. If you move farther than 2' from the wall, the effect is greatly diminished and very cold nights will burn tropicals—yet right against the wall, you have the climate of Miami, thanks to the thermal mass of your house. It's very fun to play with tropical species. Don't waste the space with ornamentals!

Hickory King grain corn is one of my favorite field corns for Florida, but most "dent" corns should thrive in the heat. Space them in 3' rows if you are letting them grow without irrigation, with 1' between the plants. The field crop beds behind your main vegetable gardens can be rotated and changed from year to year. I recommend growing Southern Peas in between other crops. If you don't have time to till everything, you can grow corn in stations by hacking up areas of the grass and planting a few kernels in each loosened area. You can do the same thing by mowing the grass down as tight as you can get it, then digging melon pits to plant Seminole pumpkins. As they grow, mow or string trim around the vines until they rule the space. Later, you can always till properly and plant rows—but you'll get a yield without as much work by working with stations.

This particular half acre homestead will yield much more as the fruit and nut trees mature, but in early years your main yields will be from the annual crops in your backyard. As the front yard food forest is establishing itself, it will help greatly to bring in loads of mulch for around the trees—or to grow your own mulch by planting a bunch of nitrogen-fixing trees and planting them between the other trees to be cut down again and again. You can also use all the sunny spaces in between young trees to plant sweet potatoes, corn, pumpkins, and other annuals as you have time and irrigation.

White potatoes are hit or miss in my experience. I would grow them, but be very quick to stamp out fire ants before they destroy the young plants. They'll chew them to bits. Plant early! It's harder to grow white potatoes than sweet potatoes, but they are a good survival staple if you can learn to make them happy. You should hit 400–500 lbs on the space provided.

Sweet potatoes should bear at least 600 lbs in the space provided.

The 12' x 56' bed of corn can yield about 200–300 lbs of corn ears. Half of that is cobs, however, so the yield is more like 100 lbs of corn.

The 140 cassava plants will net you about 1,000 lbs of cassava and can be harvested as you need roots after the plants have been in the ground for a year or so. Don't let the plants grow much older than two years, as root quality declines.

You should get 100 lbs of grapes or more unless the raccoons get them. I'd say trap and eat the raccoons, but I did that one year and discovered raccoon meat tastes rather like licking the inside of a dumpster. Better to add them to your compost.

The blackberry hedge will give you about 15–20 lbs of berries. Blueberry hedge maybe 10. If they are happy, 20 or more.

Net yield on bananas as planted here should be around 500 lbs by the third year, provided frosts don't hit too hard.

Pecans should give you 40–50 lbs of nuts per tree at maturity. They take a long time to produce well, however, and will cast a lot of shade so in a yard this size you might want to just plant more chestnuts along with various fruit trees, unless you're sold on pecan pie. Pecans need matched pollinator trees of two different varieties that bloom at the same time or they won't make nuts. They should also be placed at least 40' apart as they grow huge. Of course, you could always plant a few of them right next to each other and see if they'll dwarf and still fruit, but that would be a long experiment. It works well with apples, pears, and other small fruit—why not with pecans? If I had my old north Florida yard back, I'd go buy pecan trees this weekend and try planting three in one big hole just to see what happens.

Dunstan chestnuts are strongly blight-resistant and sold by Chestnut Hill Tree Farm near Gainesville, as well as through various distributors. I called my friend Heather at Chestnut Hill while writing this book and was told that the trees start bearing in 3–5 years, though not heavily, and will yield around 15–20 lbs per tree by the time they are 10 years old. These numbers keep going up year after year. A decade later, at their full maturity of 20 years old, they will yield 50–100 lbs of nuts per tree. That's pretty awesome.

Mulberries will give you a solid 10–20 lbs of fruit from a medium-sized tree.

Loquats are about 20 lbs per tree or more. It's hard to gauge because they get eaten so fast.

Peaches and plums gave us 25 lbs or so per tree, assuming squirrels steal some.

Pomegranates bear maybe 15 lbs per tree.

Figs are about 5–10 lbs per tree, unless the trees get big, for 30 lbs total.

Pears can give you 200 lbs of fruit on a mature tree. Two pears = 400 lbs! Learn to make perry, or just ferment the juice for a week and run it through a still to make high-proof pear moonshine. Pear sauce is like applesauce, pear salsa is incredible, pears in syrup are divine, and dehydrated pear slices are a slice of heaven. Most Florida pears are hard "sand pear" types, perfect for cooking, pies, and hooch but not as good right off the tree. I find them easier to grow and more productive than apples. Plant at least two for pollination.

Persimmons give us about 20 lbs per tree. Japanese types take less space and make better fruit than most American types, plus they are self-fertile. I love Fuyu for fresh eating and Hachiya or other astringent types for eating fully ripe and gooey, like amazing pudding. Expect 40 lbs yield in this yard. Make sure they get plenty of sun or they will not fruit.

The yam beds have space for about 70–100 yams spread over four rows. Make sure you run trellises for them. If you grow enough cane-pole sized clumping bamboo stands around the edge of your yard, you can also cut 8' bamboo stakes and stick them in the ground by each yam. Yams can be a few pounds the first year or left in the ground for another year to double, triple or quadruple that. A well-fed yam can reach 20 lbs of weight in its second year. Annual yield if you harvest some and leave others should run you about 425–800 lbs.

15–20 hills of Seminole pumpkins can yield 200–800 lbs, depending on the year and the variety. Large types would give me 20–40 lbs per vine in good years. Smaller types yielded less. And seed varies greatly!

The vegetable gardens consist of seven 4' x 42' beds and one 4' x 28' bed for a total of 1,288 square feet, which is 3.5 times larger than on my smaller yard plan, giving you a yield of roughly 1,750 lbs of produce.

Throughout the food forest and around the trees, you should plant lots of edible ground covers and vines and shade-tolerant shrubs. Pineapples can grow in the shade in North Florida up against the base of larger trees and will still fruit. The canopy protects them from frost. Surinam cherries can also be tucked in and will survive.

Let's assume the remaining perennial hedges, food forest shrubs and vines and groundcovers, herbs, and trellised crops give you only another 800 lbs of berries, fruits, leaves, beans, roots, perennial cucumbers, yams, etc. In that case, this yard produces around 7,000 lbs of produce yearly once the fruit trees mature—and it could be a lot more, depending on fertility, care and feeding, weather, and pests. The late Jules Dervaes, Jr. and his family were able to get yields of 6,000 lbs on a 1/5 acre lot in Southern California, so 7,000 lbs on a Florida half-acre are much more than doable!

Everyone's yard and climate are going to differ, so take what you can use from these plans and apply them to your own yard. Remember: calories first, then nutrition! Get those sweet potatoes, pumpkins, corn, beans, and cassava going first, and don't forget your long-term tree crops when you do. Temperate climate trees are best planted in early spring and in fall and winter. Bare-root trees are very good for Central and North Florida. Be sure to look up your local "chill hours" so you can choose appropriate species.

Buying from local nurseries is best, but I have had great luck with trees from Peaceful Valley (Grow Organic) in California, as well as trees from Burnt Ridge Nursery as well as Woodlanders for rare species. In South Florida, Spyke's Grove Nursery is a good one, and ECHO in Ft. Myers is excellent. There are lots of nurseries in Davie, Florida with exotic fruit trees, as well as the Rare Fruit and Vegetable Council of Broward County which has sales. Just Fruits and Exotics is another great nursery up in the panhandle. There is also a nursery run by my friend Josh Jamison at H.E.A.R.T. in Lake Wales. In Micanopy, the Mosswood Farm Store is a rocking place with great bread to boot, and Blue Star Nursery in Hawthorne is excellent, as is Chestnut Hill Tree Farm in the Gainesville area. Taylor Gardens Nursery in Sparr is another favorite. Plus, there are lots of plant shows across the state that feature nurseries from everywhere in Florida—hit those up! And start your own little backyard nursery, even if it isn't for profit. You will profit just by doing your own plant propagation, saving thousands on the establishment of your homestead. Seeds and cuttings are everywhere for the asking. Learn to grow them well and skip the middleman.

At the beginning of your survival gardening journey, your main yields will be from annuals. That will consume your time, your effort and your water. Over time, however, the perennials will start to catch up and eventually you will be spending less time working for your food. The hardest part is getting started. Maintenance isn't as bad. With our current annual gardens, which cover an area of about 7,000 square feet, the worst part was getting all the marking and weeding and digging and planting done at the beginning, then keeping it weeded as it established. Now that it is growing well, we only need to spend maybe a half-hour per day out there on maintenance, adding in new transplants, pulling some weeds, and picking fresh produce for the table. The front-yard food forest takes much less time. We planted that, now we just need to wait and occasionally water in dry times and weed during wet times.

If you buy a new piece of acreage with some woods on it, I highly recommend learning what is growing in those woods before you do ANY clearing. Florida has a variety of useful and edible species that you can quite easily chainsaw down, then realize later what you did. Wild edibles abound in most woods. If you remove less useful trees, such as Florida holly and laurel cherry and leave the good ones, like pawpaw and wild plums, persimmons, and hickories, you'll be in good shape. You then have some established food species and can go ahead and add in some other fruit trees around them. Find expert plant ID people and pay them to come over and take a look at your land before you clear—you might be surprised by what's there.

You can do this. Florida is a great place to garden thanks to our year-round climate. Grow with the climate, not against it, growing the plants that want to grow here. Then you'll not only survive, you'll thrive!

Conclusion

As we reach the end of this book, I hope you are invigorated and encouraged and ready to get planting. The faster you get outside and get growing, the faster you will get over the learning curve and become a good gardener. If you're already an experienced gardener, this book should help you think through new possibilities in Florida growing that I hope will inspire you to greater success.

Do not get overwhelmed. Go outside and do something. In a half-hour you can dig a 4' x 8' bed. In an hour you can build a compost pile. In an afternoon you can clear a thousand square feet. Day by day, one piece at a time, your gardens will come together. The key is to avoid despair and put one foot in front of the other, knowing that not everything will turn out perfectly. Hey, it's an imperfect world. Don't give up.

Armed with the knowledge in this book and bolstered by your own growing experience, day after day, you will succeed. You will survive. You will be an expert Florida survival gardener.

God bless you all and may your thumbs always be green.

APPENDIX A:
WHAT ABOUT ANIMALS?

As this book draws to a close, many of you might be wondering why I did not plan for animals on my sample homesteads, or indeed, even give them a place alongside my gardens.

It was not an oversight. There are multiple reasons for not including animals. Yes, I know that a proper permaculture design or organic homestead or sustainable whatever generally contains animals. We are told to run ducks through our gardens to control slugs and to use chickens to turn our compost. Goats will control weeds and cows will provide us with wheelbarrows of manure for the gardens. Nature was designed as a perfect balance of plants and animals, yet finding that balance on a small homestead is not at all easy. On a larger farm it makes sense to set aside pasture and raise some animals, but most of us do not have that much land. The largest homestead I have owned was a single acre. We currently live on a half-acre. Again and again people ask me, "When will you get chickens?" or "Why don't you have goats?"

I have a suspicion that people simply love animals and therefore seek to include them even when the economics don't line up. Human thinking is a tricky thing. We often have an end in mind, and then concoct a string of reasoning that justifies that end.

If you love the idea of some fat hens with cute, fluffy chicks, it is an easy thing to justify that idea with a string of reasoning that seems to make sense. "They'll turn garden beds and make manure and make eggs and maybe even provide us with some meat!"

I understand. I have run the same lines of reasoning in my head time and time again. And what I've found is that even chickens don't make sense on our homestead.

Let's ask the question from a disinterested standpoint, without considering the cuteness of fluffy chicks or the Instagram cred you get from posing with Buff Orpingtons.

Are the eggs and meat you get worth the cost of a coop, the cost of feed, and the cost of time it takes to manage a flock?

I kept chickens for almost a decade and, despite my best attempts, thus far the answer is...

Wait for it. Let's run through the economics.

A Coop Costs Money

If you have predators, you can't just throw up some 2x4s and chicken wire. No, you need hardware cloth, impregnable walls and roof, and maybe even a concrete floor.

If you're lucky, handy, and a good scavenger, you might spend about $200-$300 for a solid little chicken coop. If you're not, you spend a couple times that.

You can buy great farm eggs for $6.00 per dozen.

That's fifty cents an egg. That means the chickens in a $250.00 coop must produce 500 eggs to pay off their real estate.

But wait... there's more!

Chicken Feed Has a Price

A 50 lb bag of commercial chicken feed costs around $16.00. Each laying hen will consume around a 1/4 lb of feed per day. In 200 days, you'll need to buy another bag. If you have ONE bird, that is. It works out to about $0.08 of feed per bird, per day. That's not so bad. Yet if you're going for self-sufficiency, you're not in a good place because your chicken feed is coming from outside your farm. If a disruption in supply lines occurs you'll be stuck sharing your rice and beans stash with hungry birds. Our modern breeds of birds aren't very good at living off the land. We tried all kinds of options to feed our flock of a dozen birds on our one-acre homestead. They got to turn the compost pile and hunt bugs. We grew corn, amaranth and moringa for them. We tried the "maggot bucket" approach (it was horrid). We tried letting them free-range. I even fed them boiled air-potato bulbils. And despite our best efforts, their laying dropped to almost zero when they did not have purchased feed. It's very hard to get them the proper balance of protein to keep them laying. So you buy feed and they go back to laying, shelling out that 8 cents per day, per bird. That came out to about a dollar a day for our flock of 12. Assuming you can keep getting cheap feed, that's still not that bad. Maybe you just want to go ahead and do that and just eat the chickens if the supply lines break. That's reasonable. But...

Your Time Also Has a Price

What is your time worth? $7.50 per hour? $15? $50?

If you were Donald Trump, it wouldn't make sense to keep chickens unless you wanted to do so as a hobby. Chickens are certainly better company than Congressmen and have higher IQs, so I could understand if he did decide to raise a flock, but still—the value of his time is high.

But we're talking about your time or my time. Let's say it's worth $15 per hour.

You need to build a coop, buy feed, let the chickens in and out, collect eggs, feed and water the birds, plus hunt predators.

Taking care of a flock doesn't take all that much time, usually. Maybe a quarter hour a day.

That works out to 1.75 hours per week, or $26.25 of your time at $15 per hour.

At that rate, you could easily buy a dozen eggs every two days from a local organic chicken farm—and keep your time.

You might decide keeping chickens makes sense for you even after these numbers, but...

It Gets Worse

What about deaths from predators? In Florida, EVERYTHING likes to eat chickens, from hawks to your neighbor's dogs.

Going out to the coop in the middle of the night after being woken up by the dying squawks of a murdered rooster isn't fun. Discovering the fox that killed the cock has also murdered all your pullets is even less so.

At one of our homesteads, rats dug under the wire around the coop and killed our chicks. I posted the video explaining our problem on YouTube and a lot of people suggested building a stronger coop, poisoning the rats, raising the chicks off the ground, etc.

Yet that costs more money. Why would I spend the time and effort when I can just buy eggs from down the road for a few bucks a dozen? At that point we were renting so it really didn't make sense. Now if I were to build a coop, I would make it predator-proof right from the beginning. Don't get me wrong on this—I like raising chickens. It's wonderful to take little children out to the coop in the morning to gather eggs. I rather like feeding hornworms and insects to my hens.

Yet the question remains, cold and hard.

Are Chickens Worth It?

I've raised chickens for eggs and meat and I appreciate the manure and the work they do with composting; yet overall…

No. Heck no.

The "ideal" of chickens has always failed to mesh with the reality of chickens.

If I let the birds free-range, they'll wreck my newly planted gardens and often end up as predator droppings.

If I box them up in a *Gallus gallus* gulag, they need more feed and produce lower quality eggs.

I'm sure there's a way to keep birds that makes monetary sense on a small homestead, but I haven't found it. I'm no Joel Salatin, and considering tractors, coops, chicken runs, hardware cloth, feed, time, chasing predators… the numbers don't add up.

A lot of us love the ideas of birds—or we like chickens the way we like our dogs.

I don't want pets. I want eggs that are higher quality and cost less than the ones I can buy locally, and I haven't been able to make the numbers add up.

I'll bet if you crunch the numbers on your own homestead, you'll see the same monetary drain I do.

When we go on to consider ducks, many of the same issues apply. And when we look at goats…

Goats are hugely destructive and can be a big waste of time on a small farm! They eat grass down to sand if you do not have enough pasture, they break down fences and bleat at you incessantly as you work and they will happily destroy your gardens. They'll also hang themselves if you tie them up, so I do not recommend taking that approach.

Rabbits are hard to manage well. We had them for a year and then sold them.

I realize that in writing this appendix I am going to make a lot of people irritated. They'll say that I'm not doing it right, or that their animals have always worked out well, or that I'm missing an integral part of the nutrient loop or whatever.

It would be easier for me to just leave all this out and let you think I was some sort of vegan hippie that doesn't believe in animals. That's not the case: I like how useful animals can be on a larger farm. But I have to consider things from a standpoint of both time and economics, not what I wish was true. It's not that we didn't try. I tested various animals right alongside with the many crops I tested. What I found was that trees and many vegetables were quite productive, making them assets. They fed us and increased in production—especially tree crops and perennials—making them assets rather than liabilities. Animals consumed time and resources without providing enough yield to justify their continuation on the homestead, making them liabilities.

We don't want pets. We want food in tough times.

I know someone with two children who keeps a couple of donkeys, a sheep, a few cats, and a couple of dogs. None of them are productive at all. She, in fact, is a vegetarian. The animals are all pets—and not only that, they have chewed up some of the food crops growing in their yard. Did you realize donkeys love pineapples? They do, and by consuming the fruit, they have not only become a liability, they are actively destroying assets.

Another family I know has a flock of goats. They thought they were going to milk them, but they ended up just being pets for the children as milking takes a strict schedule and discipline. They consume a large amount of time and resources while returning nothing but some manure. The children will be no means allow their dad to kill any of them for meat, so they don't even get that return.

Liabilities, not assets!

The time you put into planting a big bed of sweet potatoes or cassava will be paid back handsomely. I have not found that to be the case with animals.

The only animal that might justify its keep on a small homestead would be a dog for chasing away thieves, tax assessors and zombies. But I repeat myself.

Hence the focus in this book on plants, rather than animals. We do not have a plant-based diet—instead, we let small farmers nearby with larger acreage to pasture produce meat and eggs for us, allowing us to focus on a high production of calorie crops without dividing our focus to maintain animals that have thus far required more inputs than we are willing to provide.

Just my two cents. Your mileage may vary.

APPENDIX B:
AQUAPONICS AND
CONTAINER
GARDENING

Why don't you like aquaponics, David?

I've been asked that question before and I'm sure it will be asked again. A couple of years ago I compiled a bunch of "Aquaponics FAIL" clips from popular YouTube aquaponics gardeners, then added my own commentary to it in a video titled "The Aquaponics Delusion". It went viral, racking up thousands of views and hundreds of comments before I took it down.

Why did I take it down? Mainly because I decided it wasn't very neighborly of me to use other people's failures to illustrate my point. Seeing how fast it was gaining steam, I realized I was going to have to spend a lot of time fighting other YouTubers and I did not want to end up on an endless crusade against the topic, as I didn't wish to start massive flame wars with other gardeners who enjoy their peculiar methods. Making them look bad by selecting clips of failures also felt a little mean and my conscience was bugging me. So down it went. One well-known aquaponics youtuber, Rob Bob's Aquaponics, filmed a gentlemanlike rebuttal and wrote me in person, but that was just as I was taking the video down. At least I got to meet another gardening YouTuber.

Still, I believe in my points on the topic. I think that aquaponics is high-IQ stupid gardening.

Basically, aquaponics is a method of gardening where plants are grown in a substrate, such as gravel or rock wool, that has water circulating through it. The water also circulates through tanks of fish or other water creatures—usually tilapia—and the idea is that the water is cleaned for the fish by the action of bacteria and plant roots and in turn, the plants feed on the wastes created by the fish. It's a brilliant design, but it tends to play out poorly in real life for multiple reasons. I have friends that have experimented with the method. I've even volunteered on a missions project dedicated to creating aquaponics systems in the tropics. But I don't believe in it. The missions project failed, as did my friends. One friend had his fish killed multiple times due to power outages and plumbing malfunctions. Another was initially happy, then gave up after a few years of tweaking.

The method is shiny and exciting. It looks like the garden of the future, with bubbling tanks and lots of pipes and sometimes even a solar-panel operated pump. It promises fresh vegetables and fish protein, all in a small space. It appeals to smart people who love systems, especially phlegmatic tinkerers who can't wait to get up in the morning and test ammonia levels and change filters.

For most of us, it's much more of a pain than its worth. Fish are packed into a tight space and require lots of aeration or they die en masse. Vegetables have issues with proper nutrition, as they can't reach deeper in the soil for what they need and are at the mercy of whatever levels of nutrients are flowing past their roots. If the power goes off, the fish die and you have to start over with new ones. As even some aquaponics sites note, the system isn't even good at raising edible fish at a decent price. So you're left with vegetables. And not good root vegetables, mind you. You can't grow cassava or yams in these systems. No, you are limited to greens and herbs and maybe some tomatoes and peppers. Not good survival crops! Beyond that, setting up a system is complicated and expensive compared to digging a bed in the ground. pH levels need balancing and so does ammonia. You have to learn to care for both fish and for vegetables and keep the needs of both balanced in an endless plate-spinning competition.

It's a super-complicated way to do almost nothing well, and it's at the mercy of the next big storm that comes through and knocks out your power.

Look, if I knew robotics, I could run a steel cable to my mailbox and design a robot that would run down the wire to the box after the mailman arrives and retrieve my letters, then run back up the cable to the house. It would be complicated and touchy, probably dropping letters along the way and shorting out in bad weather—but it would look as awesome as heck. Or I could just walk out and get the mail without all the bother of becoming a roboticist. Or better, send one of my young children to do it. They love fetching the mail.

I was attacked by a lot of aquaponics practitioners after my video. Fine, enjoy your hobby. I don't care to fight over it. I'd rather be gardening without all the mess and the fuss and the plastic and the dead fish. You guys can fight it out amongst yourselves… I'll be digging a new yam bed.

Interestingly, after the controversy, I received multiple emails and comments from people who were disappointed that I had taken the video down. They shared stories of their aquaponics frustration and even pointed me to articles by former aquaponics practitioners who had abandoned the practice in despair.

It's a cool system. But it's way too complicated for a survival situation. Maybe you could justify it if you lived in an arctic climate and had to garden in a warehouse or something, but here in Florida? With our weather? Just grow a normal garden and skip the plumbing. If I wanted fish and had the resources, I would dig a big pond and stock it, allowing the population to balance out with the amount of oxygen and space available, rather than trying to force air into a small space so I could jam in a bunch of tilapia. On nice days, I could walk out with a cane pole and snag a couple. If the power goes down, the fish will never know.

Hydroponics, in my opinion, makes a bit more sense. It at least eliminates the need to deal with intensive fish farming. A small system can be useful for rooting plants and growing small vegetables, but it's still too complicated for my taste. Give me the soil any day.

On that topic, some gardeners in Florida have given up on the sand and moved to container gardening instead. I have no problem with container gardener per se, but I do not think it's a good survival gardening strategy. Filling lots of containers with soil takes a lot of time and can be expensive. If you have a small space, it may be worthwhile. It's also not a bad idea if you have a bad back and want to make tall beds you can work without bending over. I usually keep some container gardens around for touchy vegetables and in places with hard or rocky soil. You can put container gardens on the driveway or a patio or an old slab and turn an unusable garden space into an oasis of beautiful plants. It makes sense in that case. Some plants will thrive in containers, and movable containers are also great for tropical edibles that can't take the frosts of North Florida. I grew coffee, starfruit and mangoes in large containers on my North Florida homestead, moving them indoors or into my little greenhouse when frosts threatened. If well-pruned, they will fruit!

One trick for saving money on soil for containers is to dump a bunch of wood, coconut husks, leaves, chopped palm fronds, Spanish moss, and other yard debris into the bottom of your container, then pack it down and cover with good soil or compost. That way you might have a couple feet of material filling up the bottom and only six inches or so of purchased soil on top. Over time, the soil will sink a little as the stuff beneath decomposes, but it's worth the occasional frustration of filling in a hole. I've found that you can grow a decent garden in tires, a washtub or even an old fridge.

Containers have their place, but overall it's hard to grow enough food in them to keep yourself well-supplied with calories.

To summarize: aquaponics is a poor strategy, containers are good in some cases, but growing a big garden in the ground is best. It's hard to beat tried-and-true methods of our ancestors.

APPENDIX C:
GROWING CAFFEINE

(Excerpted from *The Survival Gardener's Guide to Growing Caffeine*)

If everything collapsed, would you still be able to get a cup of coffee or tea? For how long? Much like nicotine, caffeine is an addicting substance that helps improve concentration and our ability to deal with life. Unlike tobacco, however, researchers have had a hard time pinning caffeine into the "bad" addiction camp. Tea and coffee are both good for you and contain antioxidants. They're also excellent when you're trying to write. Other sources of caffeine, such as Diet Coke and Red Bull, will not be covered in this book since I quit soda long ago and also don't wish to delve into what it would take to make those things from scratch. Imagine making your own high-fructose corn syrup and Red #40 at home! No. Also, if you did manage to manufacture Diet Coke in your garage, there is a non-negligible chance of you getting busted for having a meth lab. "I swear I was just trying to make Coke, officer!"

That won't go over very well.

Also, I'm a gardener, not a chemist, so what I'll share in this appendix will be based on the caffeine that you can grow in your yard or in containers, getting a healthy backyard buzz like the Good Lord intended when He invented this magical molecule.

Sure, there's some sense to giving up addictive substances that may become unavailable during a crisis. There are also plenty of people hanging on to negative and harmful addictions they should shed regardless of potential apocalyptic futures. But caffeine? That's our friend! You wouldn't want to kick a friend to the curb just because the supermarket shelves are bare and your last can of espresso is almost empty... would you? Is that how much friendship means to you?

Major Sources of Caffeine

Caffeine, despite its great influence on human civilization, is not widely available in the plant world. The two major sources are the leaves of a camellia we call the tea plant (*Camellia sinensis*) and the seeds of the coffee tree (*Coffea spp.*). It also exists in varying quantities in cocoa, guarana, the kola nut, yerba maté and other hollies, and a smattering of other plant species. One caffeine source native to North America which is a greatly underutilized species is the yaupon holly (*Ilex vomitoria*), a marvelous drink in its own right.

In this booklet we will cover that excellent source of tea alongside true tea and coffee. Most sources of caffeine are unfortunately tropical species which are difficult to grow anywhere with frost, yet the yaupon holly has a range that extends all the way north into USDA Zone 7 and can be grown beyond that with some winter protection or as a containerized specimen.

Coffee, unfortunately, is the hardest species to grow and process, since it's a truly tropical plant and has specific growing conditions for good yields which are hard to duplicate for the home grower. It must be covered, though, as it's delicious and we wants it, precious, yes we wants it.

Let's start with coffee, then cover true tea, and wrap up this appendix with the easy-to-grow yaupon holly.

Coffee

What does coffee have to do with survival gardening?

If you're asking that question, you must be one of those strange and rare creatures that live their lives in a state of drug-free serenity. Perhaps you sleep in late, eat only vegetables, and calmly spend hours watching a fish tank in your condo.

For those of us addicted to caffeine, coffee (or tea) isn't just a plant. It's a need. A burning need combined with pleasure. The smell of roasted grounds... the hiss and bubble of a percolator... the first hit of the day...

These things will make the Econopocalypse almost bearable.

I mean, honestly: who wants to face a horde of the undead or fight with AI-equipped death-dealing homing drones without a cup o' joe in the morning?

Not I.

Coffee, unfortunately for those of us dwelling in non-tropical climes, is a completely tropical plant. It likes somewhat cool temperatures but cannot stand the frost. Growing coffee outdoors north of south Florida or outside of Hawaii is tough.

That said, there are ways to grow it outside of its natural range.

Thanks to its ability to grow as an understory plant, coffee can be successfully cultivated indoors and in sheltered locations through the cold of winter if you don't let sit at below-freezing temperatures. I grew coffee along the south-facing wall of my North Florida home and it sailed through nights that hit the teens further out in the yard. That wall radiated warmth overnight and was basically USDA Zone 10, even when the yard dropped into USDA Zone 8 territory.

If you live in South Florida, you can pop some coffee plants into your yard and they'll grow without too much care. They like lots of compost and mulch and do not like full sun.

I grew a coffee tree in a large pot for about four years and it paid me with a few handfuls of fruit a year. During the freezes I kept it in my greenhouse. During the spring, summer and fall, it resided in a shady spot outdoors, happily blooming every spring and producing coffee cherries in the fall and winter.

Though I've been told that "good" coffee only comes from the mountains, I'm not all that concerned. If shipping lines fail, I will happily enjoy my locally grown coffee.

For the time I owned that first productive coffee tree, all the beans were used to grow baby coffee plants which I sold through my (now defunct) nursery.

A word on those "beans": they're not really beans. They're the seeds inside a small fruit called a "coffee cherry". Coffee cherries taste a lot like sweet red bell peppers with a bit of spice to them.

Not bad at all. Just spit out the seeds, then roast and grind them.

Propagating Coffee from Coffee Beans

Coffee trees take a little bit of time to propagate. It's often propagated by seed, which is how I had success. Cuttings can be rooted under mist, allegedly, but my greenhouse rooting experiments were all failures so I switched back to seed-grown trees even though the time involved was a bit silly.

Here's why germinating coffee seeds is a little tough:

1. You need fresh seeds

I've bought coffee seeds through the mail and tried to germinate them. They all failed. If the seeds are more than a few weeks—or maybe months—old, they won't come up. Roasted beans from the store are obviously not going to work, so finding green, non-aged seeds is the first thing you need to do to get started. I paid $30 for my mother coffee tree and then waited a year for seeds so I could get started on my future plantation.

2. It takes time for coffee to germinate

Coffee beans usually take a couple of months to germinate. Even then, the germination is uneven and imperfect. Maybe 50–75%. Bottom heat helps. I've had them come up in a month with a heating pad beneath my seed trays. You need to keep them moist during this time. I put the seed trays on a large baking tray with a little water in the bottom so they don't dry out. That works well for me.

3. It takes time for coffee to grow

From germination, it takes 2–3 years for your new coffee tree to start blooming. Fortunately, coffee is self-pollinating so you'll be able to get beans off a tree without its needing a mate. They grow moderately quickly if you keep them in acidic soil and supplied with nitrogen. They love rabbit manure and coffee grounds. Blood meal is another good choice. DFSW also works well.

Coffee takes well to growing in a pot and can actually be grown as a houseplant year-round. The leaves are attractive, the blooms are lovely, and the fruit is a fascinating conversation piece. Coffee is impossible to grow outside anywhere much north of south Florida since it can't take the cold. But the key word is "outside".

If you don't have a south-facing wall available and live in the north of the state, coffee can stand a large amount of shade, such as you'd have inside a living room. If you have a sunny window or a skylight, you'll do fine growing coffee inside during the winter months. After all chance of frost, you can put it out on the porch so it can enjoy the warmth of summer… just make sure you bring it back inside before cold strikes again. Some years ago I saw a YouTube video where a guy in New Jersey was growing coffee in his apartment beneath a skylight—and it was covered in fruit. Awesome. North Florida is way easier than that, as it's frost-free most of the year.

When you keep a plant in a pot, it's easy to over or under-water. Just give it a good soaking when the top inch or so has dried out. About once a week should be good. Coffee is pretty forgiving of less than regular waterings, but it will droop and let you know when it's not happy.

The plant itself is a glossy-leaved and attractive fellow that flowers in early spring and fruits along its stem in clusters. They almost look like plastic and make a nice houseplant. From flowering to fruiting takes nine months, so be patient.

Once your harvest ripens, you can break open the red fruit or simply eat it and spit the "beans" out to be saved for roasting. I know a guy that made his own bean roaster from an air popcorn popper and a thermostat. Your mileage may vary.

To roast your own beans in a gourmet way, go hit up YouTube. There are plenty of ways to do it at home and I'm not a gourmet roaster, just a caffeine addict. I just toast them on an un-oiled cast iron pan, stirring regularly until they are nice and brown, then grinding them in a cheap espresso grinder I got from a thrift store.

What I can tell you on cultivation: it's hard to kill coffee when it's growing in good soil and warm conditions. If you move it into full sun, it will burn the leaves and make it unhappy. If it goes without water for too long, it will wilt but usually recovers rapidly when water is reapplied. Just keep it fed and watered and it will reward you with plenty of rich, glossy leaves and abundant blooms and fruit. I met a man at the Kanapaha plant show in 2015 who was growing coffee trees in his yard somewhere around Gainesville. They're brought in during freezes, but he told me he's had great success with fruiting and production.

According to my non-scientific estimates, a serious coffee drinker will require about 25 bushes to stay caffeinated through a year. An occasional coffee drinker will only need a few. They bear more and more every year and can grow into a decent-sized tree under good conditions; however, taking care of that many trees and staying on top of picking, drying and roasting will be a pain. Can you imagine keeping 25 coffee trees inside your house? Crazy, but it would be kind of awesome.

Know this: though you can grow your own coffee in pots or protected locations, the amount of work it takes to get a decent yield in areas with frost makes this the most difficult source of caffeine to maintain in a crash unless you live in South Florida. If I still lived in my home town of Ft. Lauderdale, I'd have a whole hedge of it.

Tea

Think tea grows only in China and Japan? Think again. There's actually a working tea farm in South Carolina: the beautiful Charleston Tea Plantation which is owned by the Bigelow Tea Company.

True tea, known in Latin as *Camellia sinensis*, is also an attractive plant. A member of the camellia family, you could easily grow a few bushes in your landscaping and people would just think you liked flowers.

Tea is technically hardy to Zone 7, meaning that it will do just fine anywhere in Florida. Don't trust it to be cold-hardy when young, though: remember that the cold-hardiness of most species increases as they mature.

If you're a tea drinker, you might be surprised to know that black tea, green tea, oolong, white, orange pekoe, and a plethora of other incarnations of "tea" (unless they're "herbal" teas, which are not from the true tea shrub) are all from the same plant, just processed in different ways.

Like coffee, tea can be successfully grown in a pot and moved indoors in colder regions. A big benefit to tea over coffee is that you use the leaves rather than the fruits. That means there's not much waiting for harvest time. You simply gather leaves as you need tea, dry them, and brew away.

Tea Growing

If you can grow camellias, you can grow tea. Tea likes a somewhat acid soil and a little bit of fertilizing, but not a lot at once. I met some folks with a tea nursery and they told me their tea plants were happiest with regular feedings of fish emulsion, a mild fertilizer with a good range of minerals. My tea plants grow slowly for me though your mileage may vary. They allegedly tolerate full sun, but I recommend you put them in a place where they'll miss some of the hot Western sun of the afternoon. My tea leaves would burn a bit in the heat so I gave them some shade. Tea doesn't really need a lot of water, but more water doesn't hurt them either if the soil is well-drained. If you don't have naturally acid soil, you can pot them in "blueberry" or "azalea" mix potting soil. Coffee grounds are also a good amendment to provide some slow-release nitrogen. My friend Steven of Skillcult.com uses coffee grounds as a part of all his potting mixes, since plants—including tea—love those grounds.

Tea Propagation

Though tea plants can be started from cuttings, I find seeds to be the better option. Rooting tea takes some time, and the young plants are rather weak compared to seed-grown specimens. It takes about the same time for them to grow to a good size, so if you can start with seeds, why not do so? Seeds pop up in about a month but take about 2–3 years before you can start harvesting many leaves. If you only have cuttings, root them in loose soil or vermiculite, ensuring the pot is in the shade. Put a stick in the pot and rubber-band a clear plastic bag over the top of the pot as a humidity tent to keep the cutting from drying out. Roots will usually start to form in a few months. Baby those cuttings—they really can't take much abuse and will also suffer great damage and likely die if you move them into the sun all at once.

Tea Harvesting and Processing

Unfortunately, you're going to need a goodly few backyard tea plants for a decent harvest. The young leaves and center bud are all that one traditionally harvests to make tea. You're looking for the tender new growth. Just visit your plants when they're putting on a flush and snip or pluck off the whole shoot—usually 2–3 leaves.

And remember, how you process tea determines the final flavor.

To make black tea (my personal favorite), roll the fresh leaves around in your hands to bruise them, then let them dry for a few days and store away.

For green tea, let your freshly picked leaves wilt in the share for a few hours, then dry the leaves in your oven for about 20 minutes at 250 degrees. This stops the enzymes in the leaves from breaking down, giving it that crisp, light, bitter flavor instead of the rounder, broader flavor of black tea.

Older, tougher tea leaves have been used in some ancient Chinese blends but are no longer commonly brewed. That doesn't mean you can't experiment, of course. Experimentation is half the fun!

Tea plants make a nice hedge and in some older Japanese home gardens a small tea plantation was an integral part of the landscape.

If you can't grow coffee, try tea. If tea still sounds like too much trouble... . the next tree is for you.

Yaupon Holly

Of the three caffeine sources covered in this booklet, yaupon holly is by far the easiest to grow and process.

If you want to step off the broad road and take a completely different path to caffeine heaven, consider growing this native North American tree that's been used for centuries as a tea. Though it's almost completely unknown in modern times, the yaupon holly makes a delicious drink that contains a healthy supply of caffeine. Unfortunately, this tree gets a bad rap, particularly since it's been given the unflattering Latin name *Ilex vomitoria*.

Why?

One story relates that long ago when the Spanish first came to North America, the natives invited them to a party. At the party, the Indians drank gallons of yaupon tea, got crazy and jittery, and then vomited up the contents of their stomachs, much to the surprise of their guests.

Yeah. They totally knew how to party back then.

Yet yaupon holly isn't really a purgative. It was just used to excess. Heck, try drinking a gallon of any tea and see what happens! Better yet, don't try as you can end up killing yourself by taking in that much water at one time.

Another darker theory on the nasty Latin name is shared on the website of the Lost Pines Yaupon Tea company:

> As to why the drinking of yaupon didn't continue into the modern day, nobody is quite certain. One theory points to a conspiracy over its scientific name (Ilex vomitoria) given by William Aiton, the royal botanist to King George III. Some believe that Aiton gave yaupon this name because he was in the secret employ of the world's first multinational corporation, the East India Company, which wanted to preserve its stranglehold over the world's tea trade.

It's not fair that this delicious holly got pegged with a yucky name, but that's the way life goes when you don't get to pick your own taxonomical moniker.

If I could snap my fingers and change yaupon's Latin name to *Ilex deliciosa*, I would.

Growing Yaupon Tea

The yaupon holly is an unassuming shrub or small tree which wouldn't catch your eye if you saw one during a woodland stroll. On closer inspection, it does have its own beauty. The bark is pale and smooth, the leaves small, dentate and glossy green. Female yaupon hollies set the familiar red berries of holly jolly Christmas fame. These berries are eaten by birds but not by man.

I planted a yaupon holly in the landscaped swoop by my front door. At planting it was around three foot tall. Five years later it was a gracefully slanting 12' tree, beneath which I placed a birdbath for the winter berry snackers flitting about its branches.

Nine feet of growth in five years is slow compared to some trees. It really took a year or more for the yaupon to put on much growth at all. This is typical with trees as they need to really get their roots under them before moving upwards. Growing in a pot and then being transplanted is not natural for trees. As has been said before about planting trees, "First year they sleep, second year they creep, third year they leap."

Though it is a North American native, the yaupon holly shares true tea's dislike of really cold weather and doesn't grow in any state colder than USDA zone 7, meaning that, like true tea, it will grow anywhere in the state.

For those of you who really enjoy aesthetics with your tea, varieties of yaupon have been found and bred by the landscaping industry in a wide range of shapes. I have seen rigidly columnar forms, weeping forms, tiny 2' dwarf forms, and, as I planted in my yard, the full-size wilder form. Some of these are better for leaf production than others. You could plant a little tea hedge of dwarf yaupon trees or go big with a full-size tree. It's possible to prune for more leaf production and to keep the leaves in reach for harvest, but you may not end up with a pretty tree that way, especially if you are butchering back a graceful full-sized specimen.

Harvesting and Processing Yaupon Tea

When I harvest yaupon leaves I like to do it when the weather (and the leaves) are dry. I go outside with one of my wife's stainless mixing bowls and a pair of nippers. Then I prune the last six inches of younger yaupon shoots into the bowl; leaves, twigs and all.

To make quick yaupon tea, I simply chop up some of the leaves and small twigs and pour boiling water over them and let them steep for a while. This makes a light, pleasant green tea.

For stronger tea, chop up and dry the leaves first, then make tea. The flavor is pleasant, earthy, and much like a middle-of-the-road English tea. Excellent.

One way I really like to do them now is to take the green leaves and twigs from the tree, then chop and toast them on a hot cast-iron pan until they dry and singe to a pale brown. This creates a smoky, rich flavor that is very nice and reminiscent of yaupon's South American cousin yerba maté.

Some readers have told me that toasting or roasting is necessary to free up the caffeine in yaupon holly, but I have been unable to find any details on that. Plus I lack a lab and can't test it myself easily. My internal caffeine sensors aren't delicate enough thanks to years of black coffee consumption. Maybe I should give some green yaupon tea to our two-year-old as a test.

Yaupon holly tea is delicious. It cannot really replace coffee, sadly, since nothing can do that, but it is a good way to get your morning (afternoon, evening, midnight) buzz.

Quick note: don't chew the raw leaves—they'll irritate your mouth. If you need caffeine THAT bad, you need to seriously consider rehab.

Easy-to-grow, easy-to-harvest, evergreen, somewhat cold-hardy, attractive and delicious.

If I were to pick one must-have source of caffeine, this would be it. Sure, I would miss espresso—but I wouldn't miss the work involved with growing coffee.

Conclusion

I have grown all three of these plants—often at the same time. That's how serious I am about preserving my caffeine supply. There's really no reason not to pop a couple plants—or a couple dozen—plants in the ground or in pots. Even if you're not an addict, there are plenty of people who are. Imagine how expensive a handful of coffee beans would be after a year of folks living without them… or the value of a cup of tea when the nearest plantation is 2,000 miles away.

Heck, I'll bet even zombies would enjoy a cup of nice oolong.

Then again, *Ilex vomitoria* might be more up their alley.

ABOUT THE AUTHOR

David is a native Floridian and the author of many gardening books, including *Grow or Die: The Good Guide to Survival Gardening*, *Compost Everything: The Good Guide to Extreme Composting* and *Totally Crazy Easy Florida Gardening*. He is also the author of *Turned Earth: A Jack Broccoli Novel*, the world's first gardening thriller. You'll find his popular YouTube channel by searching for "David The Good". Finally, you'll find thousands of gardening posts and inspiration at David's personal site www.thesurvivalgardener.com.

The Gospel

As I was writing this book, I felt the desire to share one last thing before the covers close. Yes, I know some of you will roll your eyes, but if I didn't tell you, I'd be going against my conscience, so whatever. Let him who has ears to hear, hear.

Life is filled with difficulty and pain, and in the end we all die. No matter how well we excel in one crisis, another one is coming, then another. Cutworms kill our transplants. Pets pass away, and our children weep over them. We lose loved ones. Our lovers leave us. We lose jobs. It rains on weddings. And eventually, we will draw our last breath.

We don't spend enough time thinking about the end of things. We may be happy today, filled with joy and wonder at something beautiful in nature. We may have a great time with friends, having a barbecue and drinking hoppy home-brewed ale. We may be madly in love with the most fascinating girl we've ever met.

All these things pass. Everyone we know will die. The children we teach and raise to adulthood will one day die. It's the end of all of us. Ashes to ashes, dust to dust.

Or is it the end?

I believe the joys of life, the time with friends, the wonder of nature—all these point to an eternity beyond the pain and suffering of this world. Earth is broken. It is occupied by great evil powers, and all of us are groaning under a death sentence, generation after generation of beautiful men and women and children, heading from birth to the grave. Look at the wars and tortures and rapes and misery world-wide. Horrible things happen every day. This world is sick. It is not, Louis Armstrong aside, "a wonderful world". Not anymore.

We are a world in rebellion. Death arose because man ignored the Creator's design and wanted godhood for himself, casting aside paradise to follow a damn snake. Now death is in our genes. We are evil from birth and doomed to die. Our accomplishments and our bodies are dust and our human desires are all doomed to failure. We walk on the graves of hundreds of generations of people that walked before us, with the same dreams and desires.

There is only one way out. His name is Jesus Christ.

He was fully God and fully man, born into this sphere to end the pain of death and redeem those He has chosen.

He died in our place, breaking the wheel of death and sin and taking the failure of man onto Himself so we could be redeemed and our spiritual DNA rewritten. Then He rose again from the grave and ascended into Heaven, promising that all who trust in Him and call upon His name and are baptized in the name of the Father, the Son, and the Holy Spirit will pass through death into a glorious new life. There the fellowship will never end. Those who trust in Him will be reunited, children with parents and great-grandparents and previous generations who called upon the name of Jesus Christ and accepted His sacrifice in their stead.

We even know that God loves gardening, as He was the one who planted the first garden—and in the book of Revelation, at the end of time we see a beautiful tree of life growing in heaven.

Whatever terrors strike this world, whatever way we ultimately die, it isn't the end if our hope is in the right place. Our ultimate hope is with God. I believe this, and I believe if you are able to put aside your trust in yourself and your pride and your pain and call on the name of Jesus Christ, you will be saved.

It's the only way to be free. When I reach the other side of death and walk the streets of gold, I hope to see you there.

God bless you and your family,

—DTG

CPSIA information can be obtained
at www.ICGtesting.com
Printed in the USA
LVHW111045081121
702738LV00004B/24